The BRIDE'S GUIDE
to Selecting the Perfect Wedding DJ

- How to Identify a Professional Wedding DJ
- 10 Questions You Really Need to Ask
- Online Research Techniques, Money-Saving Tips, More!

By DJ Gregg Ambient

Edited by Sally Stopper

Brookside Publishing
115 Brook Avenue Atlantic Highlands, NJ 07716

Copyright © 2013 by DJ Gregg Ambient
First Edition: October 2013

ISBN: 978-0-9886467-9-7

10 9 8 7 6 5 4 3 2 1

CONTENTS

Introduction
> **Why the Selection of Your Wedding DJ Entertainment is Important**
>> page 1

Chapter 1
> **What Defines a Professional Wedding DJ?**
>> page 1

Chapter 2
> **Wedding DJ Styles and Stereotypes**
>> page 5

Chapter 3
> **How Far in Advance Should I Book a Wedding DJ?**
>> page 18

Chapter 4
> **Wedding DJ Pricing—Why Do Fees Vary So Much?**
>> page 20

Chapter 5
> **How to Research Wedding DJs**
>> page 25

Chapter 6
How to Research Wedding DJs Using the Internet
page 29

Chapter 7
Wedding DJ Sales Consultations
page 38

Chapter 8
Money-Saving Tips for Booking a Wedding DJ
page 51

Chapter 9
Going to Contract
page 58

Chapter 10
After Booking Your Wedding DJ
page 61

Appendix

Glossary—page 69

Musical Playlists—page 77

Website Links—page 86

Closing—page 89

About the Author—page 90

CONTENTS

Introduction
Why the Selection of Your Wedding DJ Entertainment is Important
                                                  page I

Chapter 1
What Defines a Professional Wedding DJ?
                                                  page 1

Chapter 2
Wedding DJ Styles and Stereotypes
                                                  page 5

Chapter 3
How Far in Advance Should I Book a Wedding DJ?
                                                  page 18

Chapter 4
Wedding DJ Pricing—Why Do Fees Vary So Much?
                                                  page 20

Chapter 5
How to Research Wedding DJs
                                                  page 25

Chapter 6
How to Research Wedding DJs Using the Internet
page 29

Chapter 7
Wedding DJ Sales Consultations
page 38

Chapter 8
Money-Saving Tips for Booking a Wedding DJ
page 51

Chapter 9
Going to Contract
page 58

Chapter 10
After Booking Your Wedding DJ
page 61

Appendix

Glossary—page 69

Musical Playlists—page 77

Website Links—page 86

Closing—page 89

About the Author—page 90

Introduction

Why the Selection of Your Wedding DJ Entertainment is Important

Your wedding reception should be the monumental celebration of your life. It is probably the most expensive party you'll ever throw. The stakes are high. A polished wedding disc jockey ("DJ") entertainer shines as a Master of Ceremonies (emcee), caters to your diverse group of guests, plays the music you really want to hear, and packs the dance floor all night long. At the end of the evening, you are complimented over and over by guests on how awesome your wedding reception was! On the other hand, an otherwise perfect evening could be spoiled by an inexperienced disc jockey who botches your first dance, plays inappropriate music at decibel-crushing levels, or uses low-grade equipment that fails during the party.

I'm Gregg Hollmann. Most DJs have stage names. Mine is "DJ Gregg Ambient." I own and operate a mobile DJ entertainment company in New Jersey specializing in wedding DJ entertainment. I'm an avid blogger and have written many articles offering wedding-planning tips for engaged couples.

As your wedding is a once-in-a-lifetime event, so too is hiring a wedding disc jockey. This book will provide you with all the necessary information to make an intelligent and successful choice in hiring the perfect DJ entertainment for your wedding reception. Chances are you have never hired a disc jockey before and may be intimidated by the process. Read on and become a more informed consumer.

According to exit polls, in hindsight, brides would have made their wedding DJ entertainment a higher priority. Many brides underestimate the importance of entertainment in the success of their celebration. To that end, this book has been written to show you on how to select the best wedding DJ your budget will allow, and about the crucial role a DJ plays at your wedding.

The first important role of a wedding DJ is to keep the reception program moving smoothly. Experienced wedding DJs understand the flow of a wedding reception and offer seamless transitions between phases of the celebration. They also appreciate the value of working with the banquet manager, photographer, videographer, wedding planner, and other key partners to minimizing any potential for problems or interruptions.

Of course, the second important role of a wedding DJ is to entertain guests and get them dancing! Your wedding DJ will make guests feel comfortable, facilitate smiles, and move guests to the dance floor at the appropriate times. Now let's get started!

The Anatomy of an Incredible Party

The best wedding reception I ever attended was a destination wedding in New Orleans. The venue was not particularly fancy, the buffet dinner was so-so, and the beverages were limited to beer, wine, and soda.

Despite the modest setting and lack of amenities, this wedding reception was incredible. Why? The guests were a fun-loving group of party people who were in the proper mindset to celebrate. The DJ met them every step of the way with the right music and appropriate emceeing. The vibe of this party was electrified with the bride, groom, and guests packing the dance floor from the first opportunity. With nightfall, a dazzling light show kicked in, and the dance circles grew even more fun and outrageous. Time flew by, and at the end of the night there was a bittersweet feeling of wanting more—the proverbial party you wish would never end.

Guests who attend an epic wedding reception will savor the fun forever. Years later, they may not recall the food or the decorations, but they will remember the fun they had on the dance floor, celebrating with their closest friends and family!

Wedding DJ Raves

The following are three real-life reviews from brides who describe the value a DJ brought to their celebration:

Rave #1

"We were very happy with Ambient DJ. Gregg and Brian were awesome! From the beginning, they were well-prepared, professional, and accommodating when helping us plan our wedding. They listened to our every request and were flexible in all aspects. They rocked our reception with great music that totally matched our musical style. Everyone had such a great time, the dance floor was packed, and the night was topped off by a couple of encore songs (as requested by guests) at the end of the reception!"

Rave #2

"All of our friends and family still won't shut up about how amazing the music was. My legs are still so sore from dancing that I can't make it up and down the stairs to the subway without considerable effort. DJ Spinz is a rock star and I can't thank you enough for the stupendous job you all did. Not a single complaint or thing I would change if we had to do it all over."

Rave #3

"Mike Wieder and Emilio Thorpe of Ultimate Sounds DJs are the most talented DJs/Entertainers we know. They came to us highly recommended, and they lived up to their expectations—and then some. Our reception was a dream come true thanks to them. Between the candlelit first dance, photo booth, awesome music, high-energy DJ'ing, and the custom monogram, our reception will be talked about for a long time. We had a packed dance floor with smiles all night long. Their energy was contagious. Our guests are still raving about it! We are thankful we went with them, and will definitely be using them for future events. They know how to throw a rocking party! We thank them both for showing us the time of our life...unforgettable."

Wedding DJ Wipeouts

These next three brides were unhappy with their wedding DJ entertainment. These negative experiences could have been avoided with better research.

Rant #1

"Oh my God !! Our DJ was the worst. He was a friend of my Maid of Honor. She said he was good, so I hired him. Though the music was decent, everybody hated him. He was obnoxious and rude on the microphone. I guess he thought his jokes were funny, but this was my wedding! My husband asked him to stop talking."

Rant #2

"A friend told us about this guy who DJ'd "on the side." He was a fraction of the cost of other companies. We found out why when he started hitting on the single girls during the bouquet toss. He did many inappropriate things that were completely embarrassing. We learned our lesson. Unfortunately, we can't go back and do it again the right way!"

Rant #3

"The DJ we received from this company was a different DJ than who we were told we would have. We met with him two days before our wedding, and he seemed confident that he would do a good job. However, during our reception, he played the wrong wedding party entrance song, mispronounced the names of my mother, Maid of Honor, and Best Man. He sounded unprepared and unprofessional. He barely spoke for the rest of the evening, and failed to announce our cake cutting...half the guests missed it. I would never recommend this company to ANYONE."

Chapter 1

What Defines a Professional Wedding DJ?

Your wedding is more than just a party, regardless of how formal or laid-back it is. It is a once-in-a-lifetime celebration you will cherish for years to come. Therefore, it is in your best interest to enlist the services of a professional DJ. Yet, some couples engage the services of a family friend who's only recently begun performing as a DJ, while others opt for the lowest-priced DJ. Unfortunately, the adage "You get what you pay for" usually holds true.

The term "professional wedding DJ" is frequently used but difficult to quantify. In most states, there is no licensing requirement to become a disc jockey. In theory, anybody with a laptop computer and basic sound system could declare themselves a professional DJ and book private parties.

My definition of a "professional wedding DJ" is an experienced mobile DJ entertainer who has carefully studied and trained to deliver a high-quality entertainment experience at a wedding.

Refer to the following list to assist you in understanding

the difference between a "professional" and an "amateur" wedding DJ.

Characteristics of a Professional Wedding DJ

- Has performed at dozens, if not hundreds of wedding receptions
- Uses professional audio equipment (brands such as Pioneer, Rane, Denon, Numark, Shure, Sennheiser, Mackie, JBL, EV, QSC)
- Carries back-up equipment to events
- Is a member of professional organizations and attends continuing-education programs
- Has a professional website and business email address
- Invests in marketing and advertising
- Participates in bridal shows
- Carries liability insurance (required by many banquet halls)
- Has a carefully curated legal music library and is knowledgeable about many styles of music
- May or may not have a full-time job during the week
- Has a dedicated business office or warehouse

Characteristics of an Amateur DJ

- Has performed at few, if any, wedding receptions
- Uses low-quality components or home stereo equipment
- Does not carry back-up equipment to events
- Does not carry liability insurance (thus barring

this DJ from venues that require it)
- Is not a member of any professional organizations and does not attend continuing-education programs
- Does not have a professional website, and uses a generic email address hosted by Yahoo, Gmail, or AOL
- Manages his or her business on a shoestring budget, relying on free advertising sites like Craigslist.org
- Utilizes a hard drive of music that was acquired from a friend or illegal filesharing site. These songs are recorded at a variety of bit rates, including some that sound muddy, recorded at below "CD Quality."
- May or may not have a full-time job

A Word on Music Libraries

Some disc jockeys may represent themselves as professionals because they have massive song libraries. For example, I've heard DJs boast about their 100,000 or even 1,000,000- song libraries! For younger disc jockeys in particular, a huge song count is a red flag that they have been using illegal file-sharing sites or copied a hard drive. A legal music library of 100,000 songs would take many years to curate and cost up to $100,000 assuming a cost of $1 per song.

A Word About Weekend DJs

It is a fact that many professional DJs hold full-time jobs during the week. Should these DJs be viewed negatively versus full-time DJs who focus solely on mobile DJ entertainment? No. So long as the weekend warrior DJ performs regularly and is dedicated to his or her craft, service quality should meet high standards. In fact, some of the most talented DJs I know hold full-time jobs during the week in diverse industries such as law enforcement, education, finance, and transportation.

Chapter 2

Wedding DJ Styles and Stereotypes

Now that you know the difference between a professional DJ and an amateur DJ, let's talk about the different styles of professional mobile DJ entertainers. Your selected wedding DJ may clearly associate with one of these listed styles, or be a hybrid of the various styles.

The Interactive Emcee—The interactive emcee is much more than a DJ who cooly sits in the booth and plays music. He is an entertainer who engages guests and moves throughout the room while leading games and line dances. Weddings with an interactive emcee tend to feature more personal connections with guests while working the room and talking on the microphone. For an example of a successful interactive emcee, read an interview with a DJ Times magazine "DJ of the Year" Steve Moody, which immediately follows this section.

The Mixologist—This style of DJ is more comfortable in the DJ booth than in the crowd with guests. These talented DJs will be adept at blending, mixing and perhaps even scratching tracks so your dancers never miss a step. What this DJ lacks in guest interaction, he or she makes up for with strong stage presence and hot dance mixes that speak for themselves.

The Librarian—The librarian-style DJ has virtually no presence, standing or even sitting at the DJ table. Announcements are made from the DJ table, and the individual focuses on executing the evening's playlist with basic song transitions. The librarian is so quiet, you barely recognize he is there.

Event-Production-Focused—These wedding DJs focus on creating a multi-media show with production elements such as intelligent lighting, plasma screens, ambient uplighting, custom monograms, pinspotting, pipe and drape, and special effects. These beautiful effects are an integral part of the entertainment. For an example, read the interview with production-focused lighting specialist DJ Steve Cie, following this section. (The Glossary in the Appendix contains definitions of technical terms.)

In researching wedding DJs, give careful consideration to style. Weddings you have attended as a guest can provide insight on the style of entertainment you desire for your own wedding.

Many couples aren't sure what they want in terms of style, but are very clear on what they do NOT want. The usual offender is the "cheesy" wedding DJ who talks too much on the microphone and runs through line dance after line dance. Read on to learn about the five biggest complaints against wedding DJs.

The 5 Biggest Complaints Against Wedding DJs

1) **The Obnoxious, Cheesy DJ**—A fun and witty DJ entertainer is an asset to your wedding reception. An outrageous, over-the-top, obnoxious emcee who shouts into the microphone and craves attention is not. Cheesiness refers to a presentation style stuck in the past with dated performance techniques and self-centered, insincere showmanship.

2) **Plays the Music Way Too Loud**—When guests cannot hear one another speaking at the dinner table, the music is too loud. Later in the evening, it is expected the DJ will "pump up the volume" for the most energetic dancing so that dancers can feel music. However, the music should not make guests feel uncomfortable for the duration of the reception. You should never leave a wedding reception with ringing in your ears. It's a wedding reception, not a rock concert!

3) **Inappropriate Programming**—A wedding reception is a celebration that combines romance with fun. Depending on the group, raunchy bar rock and explicit hip-hop may not be suitable for such an occasion. Similarly, most guests will not enjoy four hours of continuous, pounding "four on the floor" club music. Rookie DJs who are not well-versed in music history may flounder when they can't program appropriately for your diverse group of party guests who range in age from 8 to 80.

4) **The DJ Ignored My Playlist**—Couples typically prepare a list of "must play" and "play if possible songs." They

may also provide a "do not playlist." Yet, some DJs will ignore the playlist and resort to their preferred set lists and canned routines. Even worse is when a DJ entertainer fails to prepare special dances like the father-daughter dance.

5) Bait-and-Switch Staffing Model—"Multi-Op" or "multi-operator" DJ companies employ numerous DJs ranging in style and experience. Unscrupulous operators book an experienced entertainer, but then switch the star performer with a less experienced DJ. Worse are companies who greedily collect fees sub-contracting jobs to DJs whom they know little about, potentially jeopardizing your once-in-a-lifetime celebration.

DJ Myths and Stereotypes

In the 1980s, bands ruled and disc jockeys were a rare breed. Disc jockeys spun on vinyl, hauling back-breaking crates of records to gigs.

Fast forward to 2013. Nearly all DJs perform from a laptop computer using digital MP3 files. Equipment costs have plummeted, and professional DJ gear is readily available at retailers like Best Buy. As a result, the supply of disc jockeys (and so-called "Wedding DJs") has increased exponentially. For example, in my beloved home state of New Jersey, an estimated 3,000-plus mobile disc jockeys are competing for private parties and the 45,000 or so wedding receptions that occur in the state each year. It is not an exaggeration when I say nearly everybody is a DJ or knows a DJ.

DJs have various myths and stereotypes associated with them. It is important for couples to differentiate between what is factual and what is false about such stereotypes when selecting a DJ. Some of the most frequently referenced stereotypes are explored below:

"All wedding DJ entertainers are alike." This stereotype is absolutely false! A wedding reception is a highly choreographed celebration with many important details. Skill, experience, and style are critical. An experienced wedding DJ will excel over a DJ who is accustomed to only performing in clubs. It would be a mistake to view a wedding DJ as a commodity who should be acquired at the lowest cost. In fact, I would advise couples to hire the best wedding DJ they can afford. Just as the cheapest surgeon is not your best option for an operation, the cheapest wedding DJ is not necessarily the best choice for your wedding.

"Wedding DJs have an easy job." While the work of a wedding DJ is fun and even glamorous at times, it is not easy. Imagine walking into a room of 150 people who you've just met, ranging in age from 8 to 80, and being given the task of keeping this diverse group happy for four hours. A DJ is responsible for making your reception flow seamlessly so guests are never confused or bored. Performing at "once-in-a-lifetime" events like weddings also imposes the pressure of getting it right, since there are no "do-overs" if mistakes are made. DJs know the stakes are high and do everything in their power to execute a memorable yet flawless event.

"Wedding DJs look a certain way." There is a persistent stereotype that wedding DJs are male, dark, and handsome. In fact, the industry is incredibly diverse these days, spanning both male and female performers with varying ages, appearances, and specialties. Clients should focus on skill, talent, and experience, not on pre-conceived notions of what a DJ should look like.

"Weddings DJs are overcompensated and lazy." In the golden age of disc jockeys, performers could earn a fat check on Saturday night, and possibly enjoy a week of golf and tanning. Today's new-age disc jockey operates in a hyper-competitive landscape with fast-changing technology. Now DJ company owners must maintain a website and numerous advertising initiatives. Sales, marketing and client consultations consume many hours during weekdays while the weekends are filled with performances. Professional DJs are also active in continuing education, annual conferences, seminars, and local professional groups. Building a successful career in mobile DJ entertainment is approached with the same intensity as a successful career in law or finance.

"Wedding DJs only play music." In addition to playing music and making announcements, it is common for modern DJs to provide lighting services, special effects, live musicians and extra entertainment, such as photo booths.

"Disc Jockeys hover over turntables." When I identify myself as a DJ during conversations, listeners will respond with, "Cool!" Then they will put one hand over their ear and start scratching an imaginary turntable pretending to be the late Jam Master Jay. Mixing and scratching are just a small part of what disc jockeys do. In fact, you are unlikely to hear any scratching at a typical wedding reception. Ever more important than demonstrated technical skills on the "wheels of steel" is the need for great people skills. A successful wedding DJ will be well-versed in musical programming, emceeing parties, and helping clients plan a successful event.

Interview with Award-Winning Interactive Wedding Entertainer, Steve Moody

I interviewed Steve Moody of Steve Moody's Entertainment Connection to give you a better appreciation and understanding of how interactive wedding DJs strive to make your celebration a resounding success. Steve's work is highly regarded in the mobile DJ entertainment industry. In the interview below, "SM" refers to Steve Moody.

As an interactive wedding DJ, how do you conduct a wedding reception differently from a DJ who plays music and makes basic announcements?

SM: In my home market of Maryland's Eastern Shore, Baltimore, and Delaware, I have opted for a conservative application of interaction that is best described as "tastefully interactive." As the emcee at a wedding reception, I greet guests as they enter the room and strike up conversations. At this stage, the guests may not realize I am the DJ. I am already building a relationship with guests, and later, when they discover I am their Wedding DJ, it is much easier to bridge the gap and gain their trust.

While line dances are generally not popular at the moment, when a client opts for line dancing at their wedding, I will instruct dances such as "The Cupid Shuffle," the "Cha-Cha Slide" and "The Wobble." It is important that DJs who instruct line dances at weddings know these dances cold.

Some other interactive touches I add—but again, only if the bride and groom wish to incorporate them, are table games, challenges to open the buffet line, and "The Shoe Game" (a variation on The Newlywed Game).

How can an interactive wedding DJ enhance the results of a wedding reception?

SM: A skilled wedding emcee sets the tone for the evening and breaks the ice. My introductory remarks prior to the grand entrance are delivered sincerely and set the tone for the fun evening awaiting guests. There is also a lot that can be done behind the scenes to orchestrate a successful reception party. For example, I offer some basic coaching to the bridal party by creating an electrifying kickoff dance after the newlywed's first dance. Picture a packed, energized dance floor with the bridal party members' hands in the air!

Second, as my industry colleague Mike Wieder has said in the past, an interactive DJ can be a "difference maker." Most guests come to a wedding reception with a plan to have a good time... or not have a good time. We can persuade the undecided to join the fun group of party people.

Where do you draw the line between engaging guests and "stealing the show"?

SM: At a wedding reception, my purpose is to make the bride and groom look good. I don't want to be that DJ who needs to be in every photo. Actually, once the dance floor action kicks into high gear, I am not very vocal on the microphone and only speak as necessary.

Is an interactive wedding DJ synonymous with a "cheesy" wedding entertainer?

SM: In a prospective client's mind, the answer may be "yes." However, in consulting with them, I attempt to carefully differentiate myself as a tasteful interactive performer who should not be confused with a cheesy, over-the-top DJ.

Are there any age-groups that are particularly receptive or resistant to your approach?

SM: First let me say that in general, older guests tend to love the value of "entertainment" above and beyond just listening and dancing to music. Younger guests (millennials) in some cases, are more interested in listening to music than enjoying the full spectrum of entertainment I can provide.

If you had to name one personal skill that is critical for a successful wedding DJ, what would it be?

SM: That skill is definitely "communication." Great communication skills are needed to connect with the client, to connect with the audience, and to troubleshoot problems that can arise the day of the wedding.

About Steve Moody:

Steve Moody has been entertaining in the Maryland area since 1989. Steve's flair for performance and event planning has enabled his DJ service to become a full-time profession. As a result, he brings enjoyment to hundreds of people at various celebrations every week.

Steve's efforts were recognized by his peers in the disc

jockey industry as he was named "2009 DJ of the Year" at the Annual International DJ Expo in Atlantic City, New Jersey.

To learn more about Steve and his terrific operation, visit www.stevemoody.com.

Interview with Production-Focused Lighting Specialist DJ Steve Cie

My interview with Steve Cie gives insight into how lighting and the correct setup can turn a reception from the typical celebration to a memorable event. Steve Cie is an industry pioneer and the owner/operator of "Steve Cie Entertainment," an award-winning mobile DJ company that's highly regarded for its dazzling light shows. In the interview below, "SC" refers to Steve Cie:

How long have you been performing as a mobile DJ for weddings, and can you briefly discuss the evolution of lighting?

SC: I have been performing as a mobile DJ for 37 years. In the midst of the "disco craze" of the '70s, I began incorporating accent lighting around my DJ booth, as well as overhead sound-controlled color flood lights over the dance floor area of venues.

Today, some 37 years after my first "light show", mobile stage and dance-floor lighting remain the lynchpin of my show, as I offer a complete DMX-controlled intelligent lighting package that includes LED lightscaping and dance-floor lighting, custom monogram projection, and laser lighting.

How can lighting enhance the experience of a wedding reception?

SC: Properly placed color lighting can help create a moment. The changing of the ambient venue color, coordinated with a specific timeline event, can augment that event into a more memorable moment for the audience to experience. A simple example to consider is spotlighting the bride as she enters the reception hall with her spouse. It is a dramatic effect that distinguishes the entrance of the bride from what has been customary at most venues. Another example would be utilizing lighting for that all too important "ice-breaker" dance. One favorite tune to get the guests dancing is Elvis Presley's "Can't Help Falling in Love With You." This tune is widely remembered as the love tune in the motion picture Blue Hawaii. Basking the dance floor and walls of the venue in blue light triggers this memory with guests. Red lighting effects are then used for Chris de Burgh's "The Lady in Red", providing a unique experience for guests. It almost never fails to pack the dance floor!

Are there any particular moments during a wedding reception that lighting can accent special moments?

SC: Absolutely! The bridal party entrance, the bride's first dance, the parent dances, and the toast are all accented with proper lighting. Spotlighting the garter and bouquet segments can turn these sometimes mundane rituals into a spectacular moment.

From a guest experience perspective, how is intelligent lighting better than sound-active lighting?

SC: Intelligent lighting offers virtually unlimited creativity to illuminate an event with specific colors, as well as specific contrasts of light. Sound-activated lighting becomes extremely repetitive, diminishing its value from the perspective of the guest.

What are currently some of your most popular lighting/special effects?

SC: Intelligent venue lightscaping, or up-lighting, has become the most popular lighting for weddings. Intelligent dance-floor lighting is also a very popular effect. Custom monogram projection is a special effect that defines the stars of the event, the bride and groom, and has become very popular in recent years.

How would you respond to consumers suffering from sticker shock upon receiving a quote for a high-end lighting package?

SC: High-end lighting is something you utilize for a special, once-in-a-lifetime milestone event. It is the proverbial icing on the cake, producing a tantalizing experience that your guests will not only notice, but never forget. In all the reviews by clients where proper intelligent lighting was utilized, all of them refer to the spectacular lighting which brought their event to the next level. It's the difference between a professionally produced event and an ordinary party!

About Steve Cie:

A former FM radio disc jockey, Steve Cie launched his mobile DJ entertainment company in 1975. Steve has thrilled and entertained guests at over 4,000 live events, featuring state-of-the-art sound and lighting equipment, a tremendous music library, and an uncanny personality that projects passion, enthusiasm, and professionalism at every event. He has worked with many famous music personalities, including Frankie Valli and The Four Seasons, The Duprees, and Johnny Maestro and The Brooklyn Bridge.

Steve Cie Entertainment performs at private events in New Jersey, New York, Connecticut, and Eastern Pennsylvania. To learn more about Steve Cie and the magical environments that he creates, visit www.stevecie.com.

Chapter 3

How Far in Advance Should I Book a Wedding DJ?

According to The Wedding Report, the average engagement period was approximately 15 months in 2010. Engagement period refers to the time between agreeing to get married and the wedding date.

After selecting a wedding a date, first secure a reception venue. Next, couples should focus on other key vendors, such as the DJ and photographer. DJs and photographers work closely together at weddings, so you may want to ask your photographer for a DJ recommendation, and vice-versa. I find that most of my clients book a wedding DJ between 6 and 12 months before their wedding date. However, some book as close as a month or two prior to the wedding date. A few super-organized couples may book their DJ 18 to 24 months in advance.

Experts recommend that couples do their wedding DJ research once a venue is chosen. Doing so allows you to book your preferred performer without having to scramble to find somebody at the last minute. America's economic crunch has created many uncertainties. The result is a trend for consumers to book their entertainment closer and closer to the date of the event. While last-minute bookings can often be accommodated, you are well-advised to book your wedding DJ at least three to six months in advance. The better the preparation, the better the results!

If you have not decided your wedding date, you should consider characteristics associated with specific days of the week. If you envision a late-night, heavy-dancing, club-style, possibly heavy-drinking atmosphere, Saturday night is usually the best bet. Guests are well rested and can sleep it off on Sunday morning. Friday night weddings can be fun as well. However, the wedding reception may pose logistical challenges with guests' work schedules. There can also be unpleasant rush-hour traffic to contend with. Sunday afternoon and evening weddings are riskier propositions from a music and entertainment perspective. Guests may be tired (from partying earlier in the weekend) or else guarded, worrying about getting home and ready for work on Monday morning. These observations aside, pick a date and time that matches your own personal style.

In the next chapter, I discuss the topic of wedding DJ pricing. Planning a wedding is an expensive endeavor, and tough choices must be made. How much of the budget should you reserve for your wedding DJ, and what exactly are you paying for?

Chapter 4

Wedding DJ Pricing
Why Do Fees Vary So Much?

DJ pricing is a topic that's controversial and frequently misunderstood. Many prospective clients are justifiably confused by the wide spectrum of prices for wedding DJ services, ranging from a few hundred dollars to over $5,000. This chapter is intended to de-mystify the process and put you at ease when shopping for a wedding DJ.

The American Disc Jockey Association states on its website, "Rates for the DJ industry vary greatly, ranging from $350 to over $5,000 with an average of $1,200 for a 4-hour booking. The best price is not always the best deal, especially if you are planning a wedding. As a matter of fact, surveys conclude that nearly 100% of brides would have spent more money on their entertainment and made it their #1 priority in hindsight."

With such a wide range of prices for wedding DJs, even with these cited industry averages, consumers are justifiably confused. Why do fees vary so much? Welcome to "DJ Economics 101."

Base Price

The prices charged by a DJ entertainment company are directly related to the costs incurred in operating their business and in producing a particular show.

Let's start with the assumption that every DJ is in business to earn a profit. Thus, every DJ must charge a rate above their cost of providing the service. Imagine a college student who decides to use his laptop computer and home stereo equipment to launch a wedding DJ service. Furthermore, this rookie DJ copies his friend's computer hard drive, instantly acquiring a 50,000-song music library for free. Next, he finds a free service to host his website and attract clients. This DJ's costs are virtually zero, meaning that any rate charged for his DJ services will be profitable and compare favorably to the alternative of flipping burgers at a fast food restaurant for $8 an hour.

Consider a scenario involving a part-time mobile DJ who holds a salaried Monday to Friday job that provides health insurance and a retirement savings account. This individual runs a professional DJ operation, administrating the business in the evenings and performing on weekends. Overall, his costs are on the lower side, indicating that he can afford to charge lower prices.

Full-time professional DJ entertainment companies incur expenses that may include office rent, advertising, bridal show fees, liability insurance, continuing education, backup equipment, health insurance, and contributions to retirement savings plans. These costs are recovered in the form of higher professional rates.

Based on these examples, it is clear that a DJ's business structure directly influences the price quoted for his wedding services. Another important factor is the cost of producing a specific event.

Understand the Pricing for Your Particular Package

The cost of producing a particular package is an important determinant of its price. Events that require several crewmembers from the DJ company are more expensive. Intelligent lighting and special effects can also dramatically increase the cost of your service.

On the labor side, one popular arrangement is a two-person DJ plus Emcee tag team. Some DJ companies that focus on smaller weddings of 75 to 150 guests utilize a single professional entertainer who serves as both the DJ and Emcee. With a wireless microphone, this DJ can leave the booth and coordinate the flow of events as needed. In fact, this is how I perform at an estimated 80 percent of the weddings I book.

For those receptions with heavy production elements including extras like plasma TVs, trussing, and intelligent lighting, your DJ company may be sending five or more staff members in multiple vehicles. Lighting equipment in particular is expensive, and that cost must be built into the price of the service.

DJ packages run the gamut from simple to elaborate. The components of a wedding DJ package will impact the cost. Below is a checklist of the components that could be incorporated into a wedding DJ package:

- Reception Service (4 hours)
- Cocktail Hour Service
- Ceremony Service
- Basic LED Lighting
- Intelligent Lighting
- Plasma Screens
- Additional Staff
- Live Musicians
- Photo Booth Service
- Special Effects
- Overtime

When comparing DJ packages between companies, be sure to conduct an apples-to-apples comparison. A $2,500 wedding DJ package with "the works" may provide you more value than a $500 package for a single DJ with no dance-floor lighting.

Supply-Demand Factors in Local Markets

Supply-demand factors in local market areas also influence pricing. On the demand side, income levels vary widely across geographic markets. For example, here in my home state of New Jersey, income levels (and DJ pricing) are higher in northern New Jersey than in central or southern New Jersey. Across the bridge in Manhattan, income levels and DJ pricing skyrocket versus New Jersey prices. Income levels in small, rural towns across the U.S. are lower, and families have less discretionary income on average to spend on disc jockey entertainment. Thus, DJ rates also tend to be lower.

On the supply side, a large number of companies competing in a small market can drive down prices. With barriers to entry in the mobile DJ entertainment industry extremely low, the supply of disc jockeys has proliferated in recent years. With so many options, clients can usually find a disc jockey willing to undercut the price of a competitor. It is important to keep in mind that while the supply of disc jockeys is large, the pool of professional, experienced DJs is more limited. In fact, the best wedding DJs sell out their prime Saturday nights far in advance.

In researching professional wedding DJs, get a general sense of the average market rate in your particular geographic area. This will provide you with a baseline for judging the price quotations you receive later in your research process. These rates will reflect supply-demand conditions in your local market area, whether that be Los Angeles, Seattle, Dallas, Albany, Jamaica, or Hong Kong!

Chapter 5

How to Research Wedding DJs

I recommend these five techniques for researching wedding disc jockeys.
1. Based on Personal Experience
2. Recommendations from Family and Friends
3. Recommendations from Banquet Hall Managers or Other Wedding Pros
4. Bridal Shows
5. Internet Research

In fact, a bride may use all five techniques in researching a wedding DJ (or any wedding vendor). The first four techniques will be covered in this chapter, with a separate chapter dedicated exclusively to Internet Research.

Personal Experience

DJ entertainment is a service that is difficult to describe via websites, blogs and brochures. Even promotional videos may not capture the true atmosphere at an event. If you attended a wedding reception where you loved the music and entertainment, then you may have found your DJ. Seeing and hearing is believing! Take a business card at the end of the night, or collect the DJ's information from the bride and groom at a later date.

Prior to contacting the DJ, take the time to visit his or her website and learn more about their services and pricing. You will also need to verify that the DJ you saw and enjoyed is available on your wedding date.

Recommendations from Family and Friends

Conversations in which friends or co-workers rave about their DJ can be invaluable to your research. What in particular did they like about their DJ? Was it their thorough preparation, transparent business practices, musical selections, dance skills, pleasing personality, "wow factor" light show, affordable pricing or something else? Are these same traits important to you?

When vetting recommendations from family and friends, you need to apply an additional level of care. Your friends and family would never deliberately steer you wrong, but they may not have the proper knowledge to make an appropriate referral. Your wedding is not their wedding, and one size does not fit all. Take the time to independently research the DJ company to ensure he is an experienced "professional" wedding DJ. When working with a "multi-op" company that offers numerous systems, be aware that the DJ who performed at the wedding your friend saw may not be the same DJ assigned to your event.

Recommendations from Banquet Hall Managers and Event Pros

Most banquet venues have a "recommended" or "preferred"

vendors list. It is safe to assume these vendors are familiar with the venue—its location, room layouts, policies, and procedures. You should accord weight to recommendations from your banquet hall manager, but again, dig deeper with your own independent research.

In rare cases, banquet halls allow vendors to buy their way onto the preferred vendors list; in other words, the vendor did not achieve membership on the list solely on merit. For example, some vendors purchase expensive advertising in magazines promoting the venue, which in turn will put them on the preferred vendors list. In other cases, there is an arrangement where the vendor pays a banquet hall (or its manager) a fixed dollar amount, or percentage of the DJ's fee, for each performance. Keep in mind that in these "pay to play" arrangements, vendors may seek to recover their costs by increasing prices for you, the consumer.

Recommendations from other event pros who you encounter can be valuable. These vendors include wedding planners, officiants, photographers, videographers, florists, limousine companies, and cake designers. These referrals are rarely based on economic incentives, but instead are offered because the vendors respect one another's work. The fact that they are familiar working together as a team may even enhance the success of your event.

Bridal Shows

Bridal shows are an efficient way for a bride and groom to meet an array of wedding vendors under one roof. Shows are organized by a promoter who finds a space to hold the event and then attracts vendors who pay a fee for a table. Usually for an additional fee, DJ companies can "showcase" their services in the fashion and entertainment portion of the show.

Bridal shows are an excellent way to research DJ companies, as you can meet the staff face-to-face, and may be able to see them perform in the showcase portion.

While attending a bridal show, you will typically have the opportunity to enjoy free food and beverages. You may also get lucky by winning a giveaway or using a "show special" offered by vendors. Bridal shows get your creative juices flowing as you imagine what your special day will look and feel like!

Enjoy the food and complimentary champagne, but keep in mind that your primary focus at a bridal show should be meeting wedding professionals and collecting information. Wedding vendors have paid hundreds of dollars to be at the show and are hoping you will stop by their table to strike up a conversation and inquire about services. Keep an open mind, and meet as many vendors as possible. Depending on how busy the show floor is, you may only have time to ask a few strategic questions. But if the show is slow, feel free to have an extended conversation. Remember to ask the DJ if he is offering any exclusive show specials.

A promoter will generally limit the amount of DJ companies at a show to three or four, one or two of these will perform live at the showcase. Stop by the tables of the no-showcasing DJ companies as well. They may have video clips or other promotional materials to share with you. They may deliberately have opted not to showcase because they are not the interactive, "Electric Slide" type of DJs.

Chapter 6

How to Research Wedding DJs Using the Internet

A 2011 survey by TheKnot.com and WeddingChannel.com revealed that 93 percent of brides use the Internet regularly for wedding planning and visited an average of four different bridal sites during the planning process. As many as 63 percent of brides research vendor listings online. The reality is that after a bride announces her engagement to family and friends, she is super-excited to begin planning and immediately hits the Internet.

Internet Searches

Google.com is the premier search engine in the United States and a great place to start an Internet search. Once you've arrived on Google, try running a variety of searches. Let's assume that the bride is based in Miami, Florida. Listed below are suggested search terms:

- "DJs in Miami"
- "DJs in Southern Florida"
- "Wedding DJ Miami"
- "Wedding Disc Jockey Miami"
- "Miami Wedding DJs"

- "Wedding DJ Southern Florida"
- "Hiring a DJ in Miami"
- "Wedding Entertainment Florida"
- "Best Wedding DJ in Miami"
- "Affordable Wedding DJ Miami"
- "Cheap Wedding DJ Miami"
- "Reviews of Wedding DJs in Miami"
- "Wedding DJ 33132" (Miami ZIP code)

As an example, let's use the search term "Miami Wedding DJ." This search term generates a mind-boggling 12,700,000 results! In reality, most consumers will not explore past the first page of search results. Wedding vendors compete fiercely to appear on the first page of Google search results either organically or through paid advertisements. It's prime real estate.

Looking at the first page of results from this search, at the top left, you will first see several companies whose links are contained in a box shaded in pale yellow. These ads are "paid ads"—a DJ company pays Google or one of its affiliated companies a fee to be featured at the top of results for certain search terms. These websites did not necessarily have the best or most relevant content. They paid to be at the top of the search results, and are often national companies.

Organic search results are generally preferred by consumers, as they are objectively determined by Google's algorithm and tend to reflect the most relevant content. Today's younger Generation Y or Millennial generation tends to frown upon companies who game the system in order to skip to the front of the line. To be fair to these paid sponsors, if they have the funds to purchase this premier real estate on Google, they are likely serious, full-time professional companies that are worthy of a look.

Listed below these paid search results are several DJ companies located in Miami. These companies have registered their businesses with Google and they best met the geographic nature of the search.

In the column to the right of the search results for "Miami Wedding DJ," you'll see a list of companies. These results are generated from Google AdWords campaigns. In Google AdWords, an advertiser allocates a fixed monthly dollar amount that is charged whenever somebody clicks on its ad.

Finally, back to the left column, below the geographically derived list of companies are additional companies who appear organically.

Page two of the search engine results for "Miami Wedding DJ" provides a similar format to the first page, also beginning to incorporate video links from YouTube.

Speaking of YouTube, did you know it is the second-most popular search engine after Google? You are advised to try similar searches on YouTube as you did on Google, and benefit from seeing wedding DJs live in action. Some DJ companies prepare a video gig log called a "VLog" or "Video Blog" showcasing key highlights from a celebration. DJ companies well-known for their VLogs include New Jersey companies SCE Event Group, Absolute Event Services, and

Ultrafonk Entertainment, as well as Maryland-based Steve Moody's Entertainment Connection.

For an examples of wedding VLogs, check out the VLog library of Ultrafonk Entertainment at this link http://www.ultrafonk.com/#!videos/cn8d

Drilling Down into Search Engine Results

Now that you have a list of leads from your Internet search, it's time to drill down into more detail. Click through the most interesting links from your web search. For variety, check out both the organic search results and some of the paid advertisements or Google AdWords listings. Remember, those who have sponsored paid ads are often credible companies. Conversely, not all of the companies that appear organically will be appropriate. Despite Google's best efforts to eliminate companies that try to trick the system with black hat search engine optimization techniques (SEO), occasionally an inappropriate company will soar to the top of the results.

Start clicking the websites from your search result. If a DJ company appears interesting after a quick glance at its site, jot down their information so you can conduct additional research later. As you browse websites, keep an eye out for companies whose vision of musical entertainment resonates with your own expectations.

As you peruse disc jockey websites, look for the following in order to identify a professional wedding disc jockey service:
- A professional-looking homepage and interface. The site should not look and feel like a do-it-yourself

project, nor should it be littered with spelling errors and bad formatting.
- An appealing color scheme
- Fresh content—when does it look like the site was last updated?
- Photos that focus on guests rather than on gear and tacky party favors
- DJ and staff bios
- Reviews and testimonials
- Packages and pricing
- Links to social media (Facebook, Twitter, Instagram, Blog, Pinterest, YouTube, Vimeo)
- Promotional video or video logs
- Planning tips
- Song ideas and music playlists

Online Reviews

Online reviews found on sites like WeddingWire.com and WeddingChannel.com are powerful tools in researching wedding disc jockeys. On these review sites, brides rate and review their wedding vendors. These review systems are open nature, meaning that brides, either happy or unhappy with their services, are free to post a review without a vendor's consent. This also means a vendor cannot remove a legitimate negative review.

The two most popular wedding review sites are: WeddingWire (www.weddingwire.com) and The Wedding Channel (www.weddingchannel.com)—this site is owned by industry heavyweight "The Knot"—a publicly-traded company. Yelp (www.yelp.com) is another popular review site, particularly on the West Coast.

The quantitative figures from reviews are instructive. For example, WeddingWire uses a star system on various criteria with five-stars representing the best, and one-star representing the worst. The five criteria that WeddingWire allows a reviewer to rate are: 1) quality of service, 2) responsiveness, 3) professionalism, 4) value, and 5) flexibility.

Even more educational than the quantitative rating are the comments and analysis posted by brides describing what they loved (or didn't) about the service.

Tips for Evaluating Online Reviews

- Check how many reviews in total a wedding DJ has and when these reviews were posted. This will give you an idea of how experienced the DJ is in wedding entertainment.
- For multi-op companies, look for reviews on the specific DJ who will be performing at your wedding.
- Read the written testimonials carefully and get a sense of what past brides loved about their DJ and style. Look for the repeated mention of these strengths across multiple reviews. If these attributes are what you are seeking in your DJ, then you may have found a perfect match!
- Look for consistency. If a DJ company has an erratic pattern of good and bad reviews, this can indicate a lack of quality control. Or, it may indicate that there is a star performer who does great work, and other DJs who do below-average work.

- Beware of coached reviews. If all the reviews read the same and lack detail, this could be an indication that reviewers were coached to write positive reviews. Worse yet, they could be fictitious reviews.
- Beware of the tough grader. In school, we all had that teacher who was a super-tough grader. Occasionally some client couples are tough graders, harping on minor items and giving low marks. A lackluster review or two is not enough to dismiss a DJ from consideration. On review sites like WeddingWire, you can typically read a bride's reviews of other wedding vendors. Cross-check her other reviews to see if she was equally as severe with her florist as she was with her DJ. A pattern of negative reviews from a bride for multiple vendors on the site is an ominous red flag.
- Even DJs have an occasional bad day. Over the span of a long professional career, all of us make occasional errors like mispronouncing a name or a miscue on announcing the briday party. With careful prepping, it should never be more than that.
- Check if the DJ company publicly responded to any negative reviews. WeddingWire gives vendors the opportunity to respond to both positive and negative reviews and provide clarification. A thoughtful professional response indicates that a company cares about its clients and reputation.

After Conducting Your Research

It is now time to pick your favorites, check availability, and receive preliminary pricing information.

In shopping for a wedding DJ, you will likely have an approximate budget in mind. Hopefully this budget allows an adequate amount for music and entertainment, as you now realize the importance of entertainment towards the total success of your wedding reception.

When conducting Internet research, you will find that some DJ companies post pricing information on their websites, while many do not. There are several motives for DJ company owners to not post prices. They are as follows: **1)** packages are customized and do not lend themselves to standardized prices; **2)** package prices may be high and require explanation by phone or in-person consultation, and **3)** they do not want competitor DJ companies to know their rates.

As the consumer, you are entitled to have an idea of pricing prior to scheduling an in-person consultation. Therefore, on the phone, a DJ should be able to make a general statement like, "Our four hour wedding packages start at $1,000" or "Our wedding DJ packages range from $800 to $3,000." Any DJ who refuses to discuss prices on the phone, even in these general terms, should be viewed with some suspicion. There is a good chance you will be required to attend an in-person consultation at which you are then presented with an expensive array of packages and options.

An initial idea on pricing and budget is important for both the DJ and prospective client. The DJ seeks to prequalify couples who can afford the price of his services. For the prospective client, consulting with a DJ company that is too far out of their budget is also a waste of time and effort.

Prospective clients should be open-minded and consider

meeting with companies of fine reputation but whose prices may be slightly above budget. During the sales consultation, the bride may learn more and be comfortable with the "value" of this DJ's services, even if the price is higher than she initially budgeted. Another possibility is that the prices of the company with the fine reputation are not as high as you had initially expected.

Chapter 7

Wedding DJ Sales Consultations

Now that you've conducted preliminary research and narrowed down the field to a short list of candidates, it's time to schedule a consultation with the DJ in-person, over the telephone, or via video conference (e.g., BrideLive, Skype).

Before this detailed interview, be sure to check with the DJ to make sure that he or she is available for your wedding date. When dealing with a multi-op company, it's important to know exactly who will be performing at your wedding. If possible, they should also be present at your consultation.

I've fielded a variety of questions at consultations through the years. Here are what I believe to be the most important questions to ask a prospective wedding DJ:

10 Questions to Ask a Prospective Wedding DJ

1) How did you get into DJ-ing? This is a great opening question, as it puts the DJ at ease and you will learn about his or her background as well as motivation for getting into the business. Find out where passions lie, whether with the music, the emcee aspect, or the prestige of performing at formal events. With a timeline, you can also learn how long this person has been performing as a DJ.

2) What is your style? DJs run the gamut from extremely interactive to those who make sparse announcements and primarily mix the music. In recent years, there has been a trend toward "nontacky" wedding receptions that eliminate "cheesy" features like the Electric Slide. Perhaps you want a high-energy emcee who really gets the crowd going. There is no right or wrong answer, but you need to align yourself with a DJ who is a good stylistic match for your vision. You should be proactive in asking this question, as some DJs might first ask you about your expectations and then cater their answer to appease you.

3) How many weddings did you perform last year? This will give you a great idea on how experienced the DJ is in performing at weddings. An experienced wedding DJ is desirable, as he or she will have the requisite experience to preside over a seamless evening of music and entertainment, also working well with the extended wedding team (i.e., wedding planner, banquet hall manager, photographer, videographer). Hiring an inexperienced wedding DJ exposes you to the risk of becoming the next YouTube sensation after a major mistake is made. While your DJ does not need to work as a DJ on a full-time basis, he or she should be performing regularly at weddings. For those wedding DJs who are extremely busy (say performing at over 60 weddings per year), be sure they have adequate time to give your wedding the special attention that it deserves.

4) What would you do if a guest spilled a drink on your lap-

top computer during our wedding? This question indirectly asks about backup equipment, which a professional wedding DJ should always bring to an event so your party isn't halted by a technical glitch. It also gives you an idea whether the DJ is a problem-solver or quick to blame others.

5) What is your approach to musical programming at a wedding? This question will reveal how flexible a DJ is in his programming as well as what types of music he favors. How much flexibility is there in the music programming? How many songs do you pick versus how many does the DJ pick? Try asking, "If we did not provide you with a strict playlist, what are some songs you might program for cocktail hour, dinner music, and peak-hour open dancing?" An experienced wedding DJ will have very well thought out answers. Programming at weddings can be tricky, given the wide range of guest ages and musical tastes. I have often said that the art of the wedding DJ is to make each and every guest feel as though they had the best time of their life! Keep in mind that inappropriate musical programming is one of the biggest complaints against wedding DJs. That could mean playing modern club music all night long for a mixed crowd, or playing too many ballads for a younger crowd that wants to cut loose on the dance floor.

6) Are you insured? Talking about insurance can be a real mood-killer, but in today's litigious society, insurance may be a part of the wedding DJ hiring equation. If your banquet hall requires liability insurance (as many of the finer facilities do), an uninsured DJ company will not be allowed to perform at your event. There is no sense in spending any serious time interviewing a DJ company if it is unable to perform. Professional DJ companies carry liability insurance, while novice operations often don't.

7) Can you provide references? An experienced professional wedding DJ will have a thick stack of testimonials and be happy to provide references. These testimonials are probably already available on public review sites such as WeddingWire.com and WeddingChannel.com. If possible, review the DJ's online reviews prior to the consultation to get a sense of his or her style. If a DJ goes on the defensive at this question, it could be a red flag. Additionally, it is not recommended that you ask the DJ if you can drop in to observe one of their wedding performances. Would you want your DJ schmoozing with prospects at your wedding reception?

8) How does your planning process work? Planning a wedding reception is a major endeavor. In plotting the music and entertainment for your celebration, how will the DJ assist you? Does the DJ meet with you in person prior to the event? Is this planning session conducted in person, via phone or video conference? Does the DJ have planning forms and other tools to assist you? Will you have access to the specific DJ who is performing at your event or will you be working with a support staff member? Professional, planning-oriented DJs reduce your stress levels in the weeks and months leading up to your wedding. It's also a fact that the better the planning, the better the results.

9) What contingency plans are in place in the event you are unable to perform on our wedding date? Illness and injury are a fact of life, and there is a small chance that your wedding DJ could be physically unable to perform on your wedding date. Ask about what contingency plans are in place to ensure your show goes on. The fact that a DJ has taken the time to prepare a contingency plan is a testament to their professionalism.

10) Can you tell us about your packages and pricing? At a consultation, it is bad form to ask about price first, as it sets an awkward tone. Wedding industry consultant, Alan Berg, has astutely observed that consumers are quick to ask, "How much?" The question isn't because they are price shoppers, but because they aren't aware of the proper questions to ask. Of course, price is an important factor on everybody's mind, but first take the time to learn about the service. Towards the end of your consultation with a prospective DJ, inquire about pricing. By then, you'll have a good idea of the services and value the DJ can offer for your special day.

Ask these insightful questions, and you will be well on your way to picking the perfect wedding DJ to provide a magical evening of music and entertainment!

In-Person Sales Consultations

You may wish to organize an in-person consultation with your wedding DJ finalist candidates. A consultation will be scheduled at your mutual convenience, perhaps a weeknight or Sunday afternoon. The consultation itself can take place at the DJ's office or home office (if they have one), at your home, or at a neutral meeting ground like a Starbucks or local diner. The consultation can also be held in a virtual meeting using an online video conferencing service like BrideLive or Skype. Make sure you are able to meet the specific DJ who would prospectively be performing at your wedding if selected.

Your time is valuable, as is the time of the DJ. Aim to limit consultations to those DJs who are approximately in your budget and stand a good chance of being hired.

First impressions are important during the initial consultation. Is the DJ punctual? Well-dressed? Do you get a warm vibe? Is eye contact made? Did he or she turn off electronics and give you full attention? To break the ice, I would recommend spending a few minutes chatting before getting into the formal interview.

Then, the DJ may wish to make a formal presentation, perhaps using a tablet or laptop to show you a video slide presentation or photos from your specific venue. You should ask questions as they come to mind, and also consider the previously recommended "10 Questions to Ask a Prospective Wedding DJ." The last segment of your Q&A (if you are still sufficiently interested) should address pricing, packages and details about going to contract.

If you are confident in booking a DJ at the consultation, then by all means do so and secure your entertainer! If you prefer to have a "cool down" period and discuss it later, at home with your future spouse, that's fine too. If possible, at the end of the consultation, try to give your DJ an idea of where you stand in your decision process. For example say, "We'll be making our final decision two weeks from now and will let you know."

How Many DJs Should I Consult With Before Making a Decision?

So long as you have been thorough in the research and are confident in your conclusion, there is no strict guideline as to the amount of consultations you should attend. Most couples book their DJ after consulting with two or three different companies. Many couples are comfortable focusing on Internet research to identity their preferred DJ, and then booking that DJ after an initial phone consultation, email question-and answer, or in-person meeting.

Keep in mind that the best wedding DJs fill their calendars with other events quickly, and have a limited inventory of Saturday nights available. If you conduct your research at a slow and deliberate pace, be prepared to face disappointment, as some of your target DJs will get booked in the interim.

Finally, if you consult with a DJ but decide to hire another professional, it is good form to let that DJ know you've gone in another direction. This way you offer closure and will not be hounded by unnecessary follow-up calls. For example, "A friend of the family made us an offer we couldn't refuse," or "Your prices were out of our range," or "We decided to go with a band." When learning I didn't get a wedding job, I always wish the couple well. I appreciate knowing the reason why they went with somebody else. This feedback allows me to improve my business.

5 Potential Red Flags for Prospective Wedding DJs

In researching and interviewing prospective wedding DJs, there are some "red flags" to be wary of. If any of these warning signs crop up, you would be wise to take your business elsewhere.

1) A DJ does not return phone messages or email in a time-

ly manner. If initiating contact with a DJ by phone, you may be sent to voicemail and asked to leave a message. Your voicemail should be returned within one business day, or certainly within 24 to 48 hours. The same timetable applies to email inquiries. If DJs do not return voicemails or emails in a timely manner, there is a good chance they will not be responsive when it comes to planning your wedding reception. Poor communication can be very stressful on a bride planning her wedding. Particularly in today's age of smart phones and remote voicemail solutions, there is no excuse for slow customer service. If a DJ happens to be on vacation, they will leave a special "out of office" message.

2) A DJ who does not use contracts. When reserving a high-priced service, a contract is a must! A contract protects both parties. Without one, the DJ has an easy escape should a better opportunity present itself. This other opportunity could be a higher-priced gig or a social engagement. Through the years, my DJ company has bailed out many clients whose DJ "backed out" on them at the last minute. This handful of unethical DJs, unfortunately, tarnish the image of our entire industry.

3) A DJ who is vague about liability insurance. "Do you carry liability insurance?" is a "yes" or "no" question. If this question throws off the DJ or produces a convoluted answer, it probably means the DJ doesn't carry liability insurance. Without insurance coverage, your DJ may not even be allowed to step foot in the ballroom on your wedding day.

4) A DJ who is vague about testimonials and references. A DJ who cannot produce a list of wedding testimonials is likely inexperienced, or doesn't perform at many weddings. In the world of wedding DJ entertainment, experience counts. If a DJ states he performed at 20 weddings last year, there should be a trail of public reviews.

5) A DJ who is pushy and pressures you to sign a contract on the spot. A sales consultation with a wedding DJ should never feel like a trip to the used-car dealership where you are subjected to high pressure closing techniques. Successful wedding DJs are in high demand, particularly for Saturdays in peak months, and know they will likely book your wedding date, either with you or another couple at a later time. There is no need for a DJ to impose a hard close that makes you feel pressured or uncomfortable. That said, it is acceptable form for a DJ to ask you, near the end of a consultation, if you would like to sign on, or ask something such as "So what do you think?" You of course are welcome to say, "Yes, we'd like to book it!" or "We're not ready to book yet, but will get back to you." If you need time to think it over, try to give them an idea when you will make a final decision. Note: High-pressure, pushy DJs may also be quick to bad-mouth competitors. This is highly unprofessional and should be considered a negative trait.

Interview with the Founders of BrideLive

We live in a brave new world where brides can utilize technology to make planning their wedding more convenient and produce better outcomes. It was mentioned earlier that brides have the option to meet with their vendors online using videoconferencing technology. Skype is the best-known online video conferencing system, and its basic service is free. Less well known, but a far more powerful platform that is custom-tailored for the Weddings and Events industry is BrideLive. BrideLive is also free for a bride to use, and there is no software to download. In this interview, I caught up with Bob Scott and Jay Thomson, the founders of BrideLive. Both of these respected colleagues have backgrounds as successful wedding disc jockeys in New Jersey (In the interview below, "BL" refers to BrideLive):

Tell us about the perceived market need that you saw when founding BrideLive in 2011?

BL: We were using videoconferencing technology to run our own wedding businesses with some success, but were paying a lot of money to an outside firm. Bob learned the technical side of the business, and we decided to offer BrideLive to the greater wedding and events industry. While the majority of our clients are DJs, our clientele also includes photographers, wedding planners, florists, and banquet venues.

What are some of the key features of the BrideLive interface?

BL: First, and most importantly, our platform is Web-based.

Brides are not required to download a program or store any files on their computer. The bride would go to the vendor's website, click on the "Meet Us Now" button, type in her name, and join the meeting. No usernames. No passwords. Integrated Voice-over-IP audio allows brides, grooms, and family members to communicate clearly with wedding vendors without needing a phone line.

The BrideLive subscriber, such as a wedding DJ, customizes the meeting room with his or her logo and runs the meeting. To name just a few of the features available, DJs can share their computer desktop with the bride, upload and download files, review documents such as playlists and contracts, work with interactive floor plans, view videos, and even record the session for later reference.

How can BrideLive benefit a bride who has booked her DJ and now wants to plan her music and entertainment program?

BL: BrideLive offers today's modern bride tremendous time-saving and efficiency in planning her wedding from the comfort of her home. In a BrideLive session, an all-encompassing multimedia meeting can be held. Music can be listened to, event planning forms can be reviewed, and the DJ can run through mock grand-entrance introductions. Let's say the bride's fiancé is not able to participate. The session can be recorded and played back to him later. The recording function is also immensely helpful to the DJ, as he can reference it in preparing for the wedding and make sure that no detail is overlooked.

The BrideLive platform is fun and allows for a great rapport to be built between the bride, groom, and vendor. Brides and grooms are at ease in their home environment. We've chatted with couples relaxing on their couch with the cat on their lap, and even with one groom who was grilling burgers in the backyard at the time!

In today's mobile world, a bride can also use our BrideLive app to run a Web meeting from her mobile phone without the need for Wi-Fi access; 4G or even 3G is fine. We even have the ability for the DJ to simulcast an event using his cell phone for a bride to view on BrideLive.

Why would a bride opt for BrideLive as opposed to Skype?

BL: At first glance, a bride may not perceive any difference between the two. However, we see Skype as more suitable for personal use, while BrideLive is a business tool. BrideLive offers tremendous ease of use yet is quite powerful. During a BrideLive meeting, documents can be reviewed, modified, and sent back and forth. Skype users must download a program, whereas no downloads are required to use BrideLive.

Does BrideLive require a great deal of time and technical knowledge for a bride to use, and is there a cost?

BL: Absolutely not! All she needs to know is how to click a mouse. There is no charge to the bride and no software to download. The only caveat is that your DJ must be a BrideLive subscriber. Many of the industry's top wedding disc jockeys already offer the BrideLive service to their clients. We are aggressively growing our subscriber base across the United States, and even internationally.

These sound like exciting times at BrideLive! As a BrideLive subscriber, I can attest to the high value of service that it offers clients. For any wedding vendors who are reading this book, I would suggest you check out the BrideLive service (www.bridelive.com) as a tool to increase the convenience and quality of your service to clients.

Chapter 8

Money-Saving Tips for Booking a Wedding DJ

Here are 12 money-saving strategies that can save you hundreds or even thousands of dollars. And none of these strategies require you to beat your DJ over the head on price by demanding a huge discount. In building your custom DJ package, keep these concepts in mind to potentially save hundreds if not thousands of dollars:

1) Use the house sound system for cocktail hour. Most venues will offer some type of background music for your cocktail hour. While the music may not be particularly good or the sound system particularly clear, guests may hardly notice as they sip cocktails and nibble on appetizers. And, the bride and groom typically miss the cocktail hour entirely due to photo obligations. Forgoing a DJ cocktail hour service will save you approximately $100 to $200.

2) Opt for a package with basic lighting. Enhanced and intelligent lighting can drive up the price of your package considerably. If the natural lighting conditions of the room are already elegant, there may be no reason to transform it into a South Beach-style club. For afternoon weddings in rooms with windows, dance-floor lighting may be unnecessary. Downsizing your light show can shave off hundreds or even thousands of dollars from your price.

3) Inquire about staffing. If the DJ uses two or three staff members in its show, the price will increase accordingly. If you have a small guest count or do not need a dedicated emcee interacting all evening with guests, a single combined DJ/Emcee with a wireless microphone is a viable option that can save you between $200 and $500 from the price of your package.

4) Ask about special offers. My DJ company currently has several special offers that are listed on our own social media and third-party sites like WeddingWire, yet most of our clients overlook them! If you were referred by a friend, ask if there are any "referral discounts." If your wedding is on an off-peak day or month, ask if a special discount is offered. The answers may be no, but it never hurts to ask. Finding these special offers could potentially save you between 10 to 15 percent of the price of the service.

5) Ask for a volume discount. Savvy pairs of brides have approached my company in the past to inquire about discounting the price of their service if both were to engage us. We happily agreed, and both brides received a moderate discount on their package.

6) Ask if there is a discount for prepaying. Couples choosing to pre-pay the entire balance of their event may be able to enjoy a 5 to 10 percent discount to capture the time value of money.

7) Get married on an off-peak date. DJ companies may be willing to offer you discounted rates during off-peak months, which in the northeast are November through March. Conversely, there is a shortage of DJ entertainment in the peak months of May through October. These options could potentially save you between 10 and 15 percent.

8) Forego a photo booth and reallocate these funds to musical entertainment. Photo booths are immensely popular, but are an expensive upgrade at $800 to $1,500. They also threaten to limit the dance-floor action, as guests find themselves waiting in line at the photo booth station, rather than "getting jiggy with it" on the dance floor.

9) Gaining an information edge could save you from making an emotional impulse decision at a consultation. Some DJ companies post a range of prices on their websites. Use this information to get an idea of average rates in your local area. If a DJ company does not post its pricing information online, before you schedule a meeting, ask for a range of package prices, or at least where their prices start.

10) Use teleconferencing in place of in-person meetings. You can save time and money by communicating with non local vendors through videoconferencing tools such as Skype or BrideLive from the comfort of your home. Video conferencing is also an ideal solution for brides who are planning their weddings from out of state.

11) Take advantage of special offers at bridal shows. Most vendors offer exclusive discounts to attendees. You could easily save between 5 and 20 percent.

12) Take advantage of regional differences in pricing. For certain geographic markets, there can be a wide range of prices. For example, in my home state of New Jersey, North Jersey DJ rates are considerably higher on average than in South Jersey. A North Jersey bride could potentially hire a South Jersey DJ and enjoy hundreds of dollars in savings, even after a possible travel charge by the DJ company. However, there may be a certain level of comfort when dealing with local vendors.

The 12 tips above are viable money-saving ideas when shopping for a professional wedding DJ. But, I would like to emphasize how important it is for brides and grooms not to base their hiring decision solely on the lowest price. Couples are advised to select the best entertainment they can afford. If your budget is tight, look to reducing spending on less memorable items like table favors or chair covers. Remember: You get what you pay for. The memory of a bad DJ lasts longer than the shock of high prices.

For evidence of the perils of hiring a cheap wedding DJ, search YouTube for the "worst wedding DJ" and view carnage of wedding DJs who ruined the evening with serious mistakes and amateurish performances. These blunders include botching grand entrances, miscuing a couple's first dance, inappropriate programming, ear-bleeding volume levels, equipment failure, and inappropriate interactions with guests and staff.

One money-saving, do-it-yourself option, the "iPod Wedding", warrants its own discussion.

Why iPod Weddings are a Bad Idea

An "iPod wedding" is a do-it-yourself option where a couple put their music on an iPod and rent a sound system, thus eliminating the need to hire a wedding DJ. I believe iPod weddings are a bad idea for many reasons. With an iPod wedding, the work required in preparation for and performing at an event does not disappear, it merely shifts from a professional DJ to a friend or family member...or even to the bride!

Here are 10 reasons why a professional disc jockey is a far better choice for your party than an iPod, listed in increasing importance:

10) MP3 files played on an iPod tend to be recorded at varying volume levels. Without somebody monitoring sound levels on the device, volume levels may rise and fall dramatically from song to song. For songs with long fade-outs, there may also be uncomfortable gaps of "dead air" between songs. These gaps of silence will deflate any action on the dance floor. A professional DJ monitors volume levels and brings in the next song without awkward dead air.

9) DJs know how to trouble-shoot their equipment. If technical issues arise at an iPod wedding, lengthy delays or awkward moments could result. For a real-life example of an iPod wedding disaster, view the following video on YouTube produced by the American Disc Jockey Association (ADJA) at http://youtu.be/bp1i8IP1NCE.

8) Pre-programmed set lists on an iPod may not reflect what is happening on the dance floor. Imagine the effervescent "Gangnam Style" hitting the airwaves just moments after guests have taken their seats for the salad course. A DJ not only plays the right song but plays it at the right time for maximum impact. A wedding reception oscillates with energy waves. DJs are masters at surfing these waves, adjusting the tempo and volume when appropriate.

7) Renting a professional sound system is not inexpensive, costing about $400 for a PA system with wireless microphone. Delivery/pickup and provision of an on-site attendant would increase the fee.

6) A rented sound system will likely feature lower-grade components than the top-shelf equipment that a wedding DJ will bring. Why? Companies are wary of leaving their best gear with clients who have limited knowledge of how to operate it.

5) Assuming the song is on the client's iPod, guest requests can be fielded at a party. However...there will be dead air as the song is searched for and cued up, possibly de-railing the dance floor. DJs not only bring large music collections to a party but will cue up and mix in the requested song with your dancers never missing a step.

4) The prep work involved for a successful wedding reception party does not disappear. It merely shifts from the DJ to the client and their appointed audiovisual person. Music must be acquired and organized in a logical manner. Do brides and grooms really want to be inconvenienced with all of these details?

3) In interviewing DJs, you may have asked, "Do you carry backup equipment? What happens if your laptop breaks during a gig?" For those who use iPods for parties, you must ask yourself the same question. If an inebriated guest spills a drink on the iPod, what would you do? Without a backup solution, the music will be shut down.

2) Your appointed emcee (if any) most likely does not have experience in running a successful wedding reception. At the hands of an experienced wedding DJ, the reception will be seamless, with announcements made on-point and guests never wondering what comes next. Remember, there are no "do-overs" for once-in-a-lifetime moments such as the announcing of your first dance as husband and wife!

1) An iPod is a machine devoid of personality and life experience; a DJ is a unique, talented and flexible individual who can think on his or her feet and solve problems.

There is one exception about considering iPods at weddings. At some venues, the house sound system in the cocktail hour zone is wired to accept iPods. You may have the option of plugging your iPod into the house sound system to play your preprogrammed cocktail hour music. Guests are typically mingling during cocktail hour. The music is atmospheric, and few will notice any awkward gaps of silence in between songs. If you choose to use your iPod for a cocktail hour, you may need to purchase a special wire to plug into the house sound system, and will need to know the input requirements in advance. These adapters are available for about $10 at Radio Shack. Also, don't forget to have somebody retrieve your iPod at the conclusion of cocktail hour.

Chapter 9

Going to Contract

Congratulations! After much research and deliberation, you've decided on a wedding DJ! Now you need to make it official and "go to contract." Policies vary, but some DJ companies will not officially reserve your date until they receive a signed contract and deposit. Others will hold the date upon your verbal agreement and then give you a reasonable amount of time to send in your signed contract and deposit.

It is critical that you secure a legal contract. This protects both parties. Listed below are elements/clauses that should be contained in your contract:

The name of your assigned DJ entertainer—Who specifically will perform at your wedding? Without this clause, a DJ company could send any performer of its choice.

The name of the contracted party—Whether this is the bride or groom individually, the bride and groom jointly, or a third party who is paying for the event, take note that the contracted party is responsible for making all payments.

When and where—The venue name, date, and time of the contracted service should be noted in the document. Take extra care to check the date and time on the contract. Inadvertent errors regarding these critical details could have dire consequences. Also make sure the DJ has logged the proper address of the venue.

Agreed price and details about payments—In consulting with the DJ, you verbally agreed upon a package and price. Make sure the price discussed is reflected accurately in the contract.

Deposit rates vary by DJ company with a normal range of 20 to 50 percent of the total fee. Deposits are typically nonrefundable, but may be refundable in limited specific instances.

The remaining balance may be due prior to the date of the event (such as one or two weeks) or on the date of the event. Prepaying your final balance means you do not have to worry about handling money on the date of your wedding. However, some couples feel uneasy about prepaying for the service before it is actually provided. Policies vary among wedding DJs and other wedding vendors.

Overtime rate—If your reception requires overtime, how much will it cost to keep your DJ on for an extra hour? If this rate is excessive, feel free to question or negotiate it. Ideally, the overtime rate would be similar to the hourly rate of your DJ contract, or slightly higher

Final balance—A broken engagement, re-scheduling, or cancellation of a wedding are unfortunate scenarios that occasionally happen. In these situations, will you still be responsible for the final balance? Read your contract to learn the answer.

Policy and procedures related to illness—If your DJ became seriously ill or injured, what procedures are in place related to a substitute DJ? Check that these important policies and procedures are outlined in your contract.

Read the fine print—As a final suggestion, take the time to read the contract from start to finish and make sure there aren't any unfair terms or conditions buried in the fine print. Is there a travel charge snuck in there? How about a requirement that you must buy vendor meals for the entire DJ staff? If there are clauses that seem outrageous or you do not understand, then ask!

What About Sales Tax?

This is a question that I am frequently asked. The question should be rephrased as "Are mobile DJs required to collect sales tax on behalf of the state for their services?" The answer for New Jersey and most states is "no." However, the nontaxable status may only apply to the DJ entertainment portion of a package. In some states, providing service such as photo booths and uplighting may be considered as rental items and subject to state tax.

Chapter 10

After Booking Your Wedding DJ

Congratulations! You've signed your contract and paid your deposit. You have now officially reserved your wedding DJ. I hope the tips leading up to this decision truly helped you find the perfect wedding DJ! This final chapter contains some additional food for thought as you progress towards your wedding date.

Should I Feed My Wedding DJ?

Your wedding venue may provide free or discounted vendor meals, or even charge the full per-plate charge. I do not require my clients feed me at an event, but always appreciate it when they do. Eating keeps me nourished and mentally sharp, particularly for an event lasting six hours or longer. When fed at a wedding, I don't take an extended break. I usually wolf down my meal in five minutes or less!

If you are not providing your DJ with a meal, give them advanced notice so they can eat prior to the event and plan to pack a sandwich or energy bar. Some wedding DJs require in their contract that they be fed at the event.

Should I Tip my Wedding DJ?

You are not expected to tip your wedding DJ a standard percentage like 15 percent, as you would the waitstaff. Your DJ is paid a professional rate for his or her services. Of course, if you feel your performer went above and beyond to make your wedding reception special, a gratuity is always appreciated. This amount could be a token thank-you like $20, or a magnanimous tip of hundreds of dollars. Again, a tip is appreciated but never expected.

Some clients have a notion that a DJ company owner who performs at a wedding should not be tipped, while an employee for that company should be tipped. In reality, both owners and employees work hard and should be eligible to receive a tip if you feel they did an outstanding job!

Reviews - The Best Tip of All

In lieu of or in addition to a financial tip, a powerful gift you can give your DJ to show your appreciation is a written review on WeddingWire.com or WeddingChannel.com! Taking just 5 to 10 minutes of your time to prepare, a glowing review can pay your DJ dividends for years to come in the form of new bookings! A great time to post this review is in the week or two after returning from your honeymoon, while the memories are still fresh in your mind.

The Top 5 General Tips for a Bride and Groom to Be

Having been in the wedding industry for some years, I know a thing or two about having a great wedding. Here are my top five tips to maximize the joy on your wedding day!

1) Keep your wedding reception streamlined. A four-hour reception party may seem like a long time, but it is not. The first 30 to 45 minutes will be consumed by formalities such as special dances and toasts, with the next 90 minutes taken up with a served dinner. Open dance time is scarce, so avoid bogging down the program with additional speeches and ceremonies. Special people can be acknowledged in other ways earlier in the day.

2) Relax and enjoy your wedding day. Enjoy the fruits of your careful planning and savvy choice of wedding vendors. If any minor gaffes should occur, let them run off you like water. Savor the joy of the day and bask in the love of your new life partner. To ease any anxiety, consider engaging the services of a "day of" wedding planner/coordinator.

3) Don't wait until the last minute to prepare a video slide show. Preparation of video slide shows is a time-consuming endeavor you should not leave to the last minute. I have seen too many clients procrastinate and go down to the wire, causing a lot of undue stress on themselves.

4) Hit the dance floor, and your guests will follow. A bride who is enjoying herself on the dance floor is like a magnet and will attract other guests to join in the fun!

5) Be open-minded in receiving input from your wedding DJ. Even if you have a very clear vision of your music and entertainment program, take the time to ask your DJ for his or her honest opinion. Are you missing something? Is there anything that might not work, based on their experience? Should you add anything?

Tips for Musical Programming

After engaging the services of a wedding DJ for your special day, a key task in the planning process is picking music for your wedding reception. Some couples are very "hands on" with the playlist, while others give a general direction to their DJ, trusting his or her expertise.

Assuming a four-hour reception and 15 songs per hour, you would have a playlist of 60 songs. How many songs should you pick in advance? My recommendation is to prepare a list of up to 20 "must play" songs, plus another 20 "play If possible" tracks. That leaves an additional 20 tracks for your DJ to select. However, the DJ will pick these additional songs within your genre parameters. For example, if you love '90s dance music but dislike country music, the DJ would keep the mix within these guidelines.

Eight Tips for Picking Specific Songs for Your Wedding Reception

1) Select a variety of musical styles. Your wedding reception will feature a wide range of guest ages, most likely from teenagers to older adults. You would be wise to select songs that cater to the various age brackets, so all guests feel like they are a part of your special day.

2) Start your dance sets with recognizable oldies. For the initial dance set, the appetizer course, begin with oldies genres such as '60s Rock, Motown, or Disco, to gain the trust of older guests. By doing so, they are more likely to go with the flow for your modern dance selections later in the night!

3) Use nondanceable selections for cocktail hour or dinner music. If you enjoy nondanceable genres such as indie rock, use these selections for the atmospheric cocktail hour or dinner music. For open dancing after dinner, this eclectic fare will likely fail and result in a thin or empty dance floor.

4) For open dancing, gravitate towards mainstream selections. After dinner, the DJ needs to quickly mobilize your diverse group of guests and create a packed dance floor. It is sound advice to use songs that are recognized by most guests! For example, young adults will recognize a classic party jam like "Shout" from the movies, while adult guests will have heard today's super-hits by the likes of Pitbull, Rihanna, or LMFAO on the radio. One of the more interesting dynamics I've observed performing at weddings is when older guests request current hits while teenagers request classic rock 'n' roll from the '60s and '70s.

5) Consider using line dances as icebreakers. Yes, there has been a trend in recent years towards "nontacky" DJ entertainment with minimal or no line dancing - you know, the usual suspects like the Electric Slide and Cupid Shuffle. That said, for the right crowd, line dances can quickly pack a dance floor with guests of all ages. The DJ can then guide this packed dance floor to the music that you really want to hear.

6) Include several ballad sets. Wedding receptions are celebrations that should feature a combination of romance and fun. I recommend two or three ballad sets of two songs each. Incorporating slow dancing makes sense because it allows your shy and older guests to join the action and, ballads are a welcome relief from extended sets of high-tempo dancing. I recommend programming ballads in pairs because

typically a couple will not get to the dance floor until the middle of the first song.

7) Have a detailed discussion about music with your wedding DJ. Professional wedding DJs are highly experienced with musical programming and can provide suggestions that will enhance the quality of your event. Show the DJ your playlist and ask for their candid feedback. Have a detailed discussion with the DJ about your guest demographics that may provide clues on what music will work. Discuss your policy on fielding guest requests, line dances, and your expectations for the dance floor action. If you envision a lower-key event, don't be afraid to let the DJ know that a frenetic dance floor is not your goal.

8) Ask for input from friends and family. When guests RSVP for your wedding, you can also ask them to write down a song request or their favorite love song for the reception. Now your guests are a part of the music mix and eagerly anticipating when the DJ will play their song!

I will conclude this section with two real-life stories. The first is about a client playlist that failed at the event. The second is about a client playlist that was a smashing success.

Story #1
Miles and Lycel were a modern couple with a love of punk, alternative, and new wave music. Their playlist largely reflected this. At the event, I was faced with a room dominated by middle-aged and older guests, as well as a large Filipino contingent. Their music picks were not working and an agitated Uncle was complaining, so I spoke with the groom,

who gave me the thumbs-up to broaden the mix. The party quickly got back on track and ended on a high note!

Story #2
The successful playlist was submitted by Laura and Billy, and featured a great mix of oldies, line dances, and current upbeat dance music. Their great musical selections united guests of all ages, and the dance floor was packed the entire night.

Follow these musical programming tips, and you can look forward to guests commending your wedding reception as the best that they've ever attended!

Appendix

Glossary

Hopefully your wedding DJ doesn't barrage you with jargon, but just in case, here is a glossary to guide you!

Backup Equipment—Equipment brought on-site to a party to use in the event of equipment failure of a DJ's primary system. Professional DJs bring backup equipment to weddings, while amateur DJs typically do not.

Beatmatching—This is the craft of matching two records to the same tempo so they can be blended or mixed by the DJ. The benefit to your dance floor is that guests never miss a step!

Bedroom DJ—Bedroom DJs spend countless hours experimenting with music literally in their bedroom or home studio. They have minimal or no experience in emceeing or interacting with guests.

Club DJ—Club DJs perform in public clubs spinning electronic dance music or hip-hop. Club DJs are generally not experienced in running weddings and other private parties.

Craigslist DJ—CraigsList.org is a free online classified section where budget shoppers and amateur DJs hope to make a love connection. A Craigslist DJ hates spending money on traditional advertising and trolls Craigslist for party opportunities.

Custom Monogram—Using a custom template ("gobo") and a special high watt lighting fixture, a DJ or lighting company projects a custom design on the dance floor or wall of the venue. For example "Amanda & Adam, 12/15/12" inside a graphic of a heart.

Digital DJ—A digital DJ plays digital music files (most commonly MP3 files), typically utilizing a laptop computer and mixer/controller to perform. Digital DJs can easily bring thousands of songs to a party without having to lug large boxes of CDs or crates of records. Many digital DJs have Wi-Fi access and can download MP3 files onsite. Most mobile DJs are digital DJs.

Disc Jockey—A disc jockey, also known as "DJ," is a person who plays recorded music for an audience. Originally "disc" referred to phonograph records, not the later compact Discs (CDs). Today, the term includes all forms of music playback, regardless of the medium. The primary types of DJs are mobile DJs, club DJs, radio DJs and bedroom DJs.

Double-Booking—An unpleasant situation in which a DJ commits to perform at more than one party for an allotted time slot. In a double-booking situation, the DJ must send a substitute for one performance or back out of a performance.

Downlighting—The practice of mounting fixtures overhead to illuminate something from above. Fixtures used for downlighting are most commonly mounted on portable stands that often telescope into the air, or from trussing, or even from the venue structure itself. Any light with a beam that aims down is a downlight. The most common type of downlight to find in an event space is sometimes referred to as a pin spot or a down spot. The term "spot" refers to the angle of the light beam from the fixture. A spotlight has a narrower beam than a floodlight, which makes spotlights good for highlighting specific elements such as a wedding cake or dessert table, whereas a light with a wider beam angle (flood, for example) is better suited for washing the entire dance floor in light or color.

DMX—In short, DMX is a system of controlling intelligent-lighting fixtures and dimmers.

Emcee (MC)—The emcee is the master of ceremonies" and the person on the microphone. Many wedding DJ staffing configurations feature an exclusive MC who works with a music mixer. In another popular configuration, one professional DJ serves as both the emcee and the music mixer.

Facade—Also known as a "frontboard," a facade is a paneled fence-like object placed in front of a DJ's table. An important function of a facade is to conceal unsightly wires and deliver a visually appealing DJ booth. Many DJs now backlight their translucent facades with LED lighting, further enhancing the aesthetics of the DJ booth.

Gobo—Derived from "Go Between" or "Goes Before Optics" a gobo is a physical template slotted inside, or placed in front of, a lighting source, used to control the shape of emitted light. Your DJ company can project a custom gobo onto your dance floor or a wall with a monogram such as "Mike & Julie, 6.23.13." Glass gobos (for highly curved or intricate designs) are more expensive than metal gobos.

Intelligent Lighting—As opposed to plug-and-play fixtures that are sound activated or run through pre-set programs, intelligent lighting fixtures can be programmed to the operator's exact specifications to produce custom lighting shows. In addition, intelligent lighting fixtures can be linked together, with the fixtures working in harmony to produce an elegant light show that is not possible with plug-and-play fixtures.

Interactive DJ—An interactive DJ is one who engages guests on a personal level. An interactive DJ may lead dances, run table games, or engage guests one-on-one. An interactive DJ tends to spend a good amount of his or her time outside of the DJ booth mingling with guests.

iPod Wedding—A "do-it-yourself" option where a DJ is replaced with an iPod stocked with preprogrammed music that is played over a rented sound system. This do-it-yourself solution is full of pitfalls and is NOT recommended.

LED Light—A light-emitting diode (LED) is a semiconductor light source. Most modern day DJ lighting fixtures - sound active, intelligent, and uplighting, feature LED lighting. LED lights will last for tens of thousands of hours before burning out, and importantly, are cool to the touch. The incandescent lighting fixtures of the past became increasingly hot, placing younger guests in particular at risk (kids are drawn to DJ lights like moths to a flame!).

Liability Insurance—Required by most finer banquet halls, liability insurance may insulate the banquet hall from liability in the event of an accident during your wedding. If your banquet hall facility requires liability insurance, make sure your selected DJ company carries liability insurance.

Line Dancing—In these group dances, guests form lines and then perform the choreographed dance steps, often led by a charismatic DJ dancer/Emcee. Popular line dances include the Cha-Cha Slide, Cupid Shuffle, the Electric Boogie (better known as the Electric Slide) and the Wobble.

Mashup—A mashup is a combination of two or more separate songs into one unique production. For example, Michael Jackson's "Billie Jean" with Justin Timberlake's "Sexy Back" mashed up to produce "Sexy Jack." Other sample mashups include Usher versus AC/DC and LMFAO versus Bon Jovi. A good mashup or two at a wedding can really make the music mix stand out!

Mobile DJ—A disc jockey who is mobile and brings the party to you. The venue provides a table and access to electrical power, and the mobile DJ brings a professional sound system and light show.

Multi-Op—Short for "multi-operator", this term refers to a DJ company with more than one system/entertainer.

Par Can—An acronym for "parabolic aluminized reflector", a par can is the lamp housing used to contain an LED or incandescent light. Par cans are used to produce ambient uplighting, color washes; or to back light a DJ facade.

Pin-spotting—Pin-spotting is a form of downlighting that is used at weddings to accent objects like the wedding cake and table centerpieces.

Pipe and Drape—Pipe and Drape refers to pipe (aluminum or steel), fixed or adjustable telescoping vertical uprights supported by a weighted steel base, and adjustable telescopic or fixed horizontals that provide a drape support frame with removable drape panels. Pipe and Drape is used to divide, hide, and/or decorate a space temporarily. The pipe and drape can then be uplit with LED lighting.

Plasma Television—Generically used to refer to flat-screen TVs, plasma TVs are used to project media such as music videos, visualizations, photos, live video feeds, and video slide shows. Measured in diagonal inches, mobile DJs typically utilize plasma screens of between 32 and 50 inches or higher.

Professional Wedding Disc Jockey—An experienced mobile DJ entertainer who has carefully studied and trained to deliver a high-quality entertainment experience at a wedding.

Remix—A remix refers to the modification of an original song into a new version, generally with a more danceable beat than the original. Professional DJs carry remixes that are often not available to the general public and that can take your dance floor to new heights.

Scrim Cover—Constructed of a Lyrca-like fabric, scrim covers are used to cover and enhance the appearance of items like speaker stands and lighting stands. White scrim covers can be backlit with LED lighting to produce a cool, modern presentation.

Social Media—Websites such as Facebook, Twitter, Instagram, and Pinterest that allow a bride to interact more closely with a wedding DJ.

Single-Op—Short for "single-operator" this term refers to a DJ company with a single entertainer/system.

Sound-Active Lighting—Also known as "plug-and-play" lighting, sound-active lighting fixtures generate a light show to the beat of the music. These workhorse fixtures are less elegant than intelligent lighting but get the job done. Sound-active lighting shows are less expensive than intelligent lighting shows.

Subcontract Deal—A practice where a DJ who is already booked then moves to "sub out" the job to another DJ, earning a referral fee in the process. So long as the subcontracted DJ is a seasoned performer of good quality, there is nothing inherently wrong with subcontracting. However, DJs who subcontract out jobs without adequate quality control could leave the client with a lousy DJ.

Truss—A framework, typically consisting of rafters, posts and struts, that supports a DJ company's intelligent-lighting show and plasma televisions. Truss stands can be dressed in scrim covers and uplit with LED lighting.

Uplighting—An ambient lighting effect where par cans are placed on the floor with light projected up the wall. Uplighting transforms the ambience of a room and works best in rooms with high ceilings or architectural features like columns.

Video Blog (or "VLog")—While traditional blogs use words and photos, a VLog tells a story with actual video footage. Video blogs are a great way to experience the service offerings of a wedding DJ, possibly at your venue, and gain a great idea of what your wedding reception will look and feel like.

Musical Playlists

There are many dreadful wedding playlists circulating on the Internet. These lists were clearly not compiled by music people, as they contain songs with inappropriate themes and lyrics, or just aren't danceable.

Try these lists compiled by real DJs and real-life couples below. Should you be stumped when thinking of song ideas for your wedding, feel free to drop me a line at gregg@ambientdj.com

All of these playlists as well as others are on my Pinterest page at http://pinterest.com/greggambient/ You can click on the pins to listen to each song on YouTube. For many songs, I have also provided listening notes.

I. Wedding Ceremony Music
10 Classical Selections

1. Canon in D—Pachelbel
2. Sleepers Awake—Johann Sebastian Bach
3. Sarabande—Johann Sebastian Bach
4. Air on a G String—Johann Sebastian Bach
5. I Was Glad—Charles Hubert Hastings Parry (used by Prince William and Princess Kate)

6. Spring (from The Four Seasons)—Antonio Vivaldi
7. Nimrod (from "Enigma Variations")—Edward Elgar
8. Bridal Chorus (Here Comes the Bride)—Richard Wagner
9. Trumpet Voluntary—Jeremiah Clarke
10. 1Trumpet Tune—Henry Purcell

10 Modern Selections

1. Paint the Sky With Stars—Enya
2. 1, 2, 3, 4—Cover version of Plain White Tees by Vitamin String Quartet
3. Holocene—Cover version of Bon Iver, Vitamin String Quartet
4. I'm Yours—Jason Mraz
5. Bless the Broken Road (piano)—The O'Neill Brothers
6. First Day of My Life—Bright Eyes
7. The Dog Days Are Over—Florence & The Machine
8. Bellissimo—Ilya
9. Angel—Robin Thicke
10. Ribbon in the Sky—Stevie Wonder

II. Grand Entrance Songs

1. Top Gun Anthem—Harold Faltermeyer (soundtracks)
2. Chank—John Scofield (funky jazz)
3. Booty Swing—Parov Stelar (electro-swing)
4. Forever—Chris Brown (pop)
5. Bring Em Out—T.I. f/Swizz Beats (hip hop)
6. Party Rock Anthem—LMFAO (dance)
7. Pump It Up—Danzel (dance)
8. Now That We Found Love—Heavy D & the Boyz (90s/dance)
9. When Love Takes Over—David Guetta f/Kelly Rowland (dance)
10. Thunderstruck—AC/DC (rock)
11. The Final Countdown—Europe (80s glam rock)

12. Let's Get Married (Remix)—Jagged Edge (R&B)
13. Bittersweet Symphony—The Verve (alternative)
14. Life is a Highway—Rascal Flatts (country)
15. Theme Song from Pirates of the Caribbean (soundtracks)
16. Theme Song from the Movie Star Wars (soundtracks)
17. Sirius—Alan Parsons Project (i.e. Chicago Bulls theme song)
18. Heavy Action—Johnny Pearson (Monday Night football song)
19. Viva La Vida—Coldplay (modern rock)
20. Welcome to the Jungle—Guns and Roses (rock)
21. I Gotta Feeling—The Black Eyed Peas (dance)
22. We Will Rock You—Queen (rock)
23. For a Moment Like This—Kelly Clarkson (pop)
24. Give Me Everything Tonight—Pitbull w/Ne-Yo & Nayer (dance)
25. Run this Town—Jay-Z, Rihanna and Kanye West (hip hop)

III. First Dance Songs
25 Modern or Alternative First Dance Songs

1. You Are the Best Thing—Ray LaMontagne (alternative rock)
2. Fade Into You—Mazzy Star (psychedelic rock)
3. Slave to Love—Bryan Ferry (pop rock)
4. Desire—Ryan Adams (alternative rock)
5. The Blower's Daughter—Damien Rice (folk rock)
6. I Only Have Eyes for You-The Flamingos, Jamie Cullum (cover)
7. Make a Memory—Bon Jovi (pop rock)
8. Marry Me—Train (pop)
9. I'm Yours—Jason Mraz (folk rock)
10. Better Together—Jack Johnson (folk rock)
11. I'll Be—Edwin McCain (pop rock)
12. In a Little While—U2 (pop rock)
13. Two Love Birds—Robin Thicke (R&B)
14. By Your Side—Sade (R&B)
15. Come Away with Me—Norah Jones (adult contemporary)

16. Lovesong—The Cure, or 311 (80s/New Wave)
17. The Way I Am—Ingrid Michaelson (folk)
18. All Mine—Portishead (electronic downtempo)
19. The Luckiest—Ben Folds (pop rock)
20. My Favourite Book—Stars (indie pop)
21. Do You Realize—The Flaming Lips (alternative rock)
22. True Companion—Marc Cohn (folk rock)
23. Are You Gonna Kiss Me or Not—Thompson Square (country)
24. Just a Kiss—Lady Antebellum (country)
25. Wanted—Hunter Hayes (country)

25 Traditional and Timeless First Dance Songs

1. When a Man Loves a Woman—Percy Sledge (soul)
2. You Make Me Feel Brand New—The Stylistics (soul)
3. These Arms of Mine—Otis Redding (soul)
4. It Had To Be You—Harry Connick, Jr. (jazz/big band)
5. The Way You Look Tonight—Frank Sinatra (big band) or Tony Bennett (ballad)
6. Crazy Love—Van Morrison (soft rock)
7. I Will—The Beatles (pop rock)
8. Bless the Broken Road—Rascal Flatts (country)
9. Amazed—Lonestar (country)
10. Can't Help Falling in Love—Elvis (oldies)
11. Saving All My Love for You—Whitney Houston (R&B)
12. Heaven—Bryan Adams (80s)
13. Don't Want to Miss a Thing—Aerosmith (rock)
14. At Last—Etta James (soul)
15. Always and Forever—Heatwave (R&B)
16. All My Life—K.C. and Jojo (R&B)
17. Through the Fire—Chaka Khan (R&B)
18. From This Moment—Shania Twain with Bryan White (country)
19. It's Your Love—Tim McGraw and Faith Hill (country)

20. Best of My Love—The Eagles (soft rock)
21. How Deep Is Your Love—The Bee Gees (disco/soft rock)
22. Crazy for You—Madonna (80s)
23. Lost in Love—Air Supply (soft rock)
24. Unchained Melody—The Righteous Brothers (oldies)
25. We Have All the Time in the World—Louis Armstrong (jazz/vocalist)

IV. Father-Daughter Dance

1. Father & Daughter—Paul Simon (folk rock)
2. I Loved Her First—Heartland (country)
3. My Little Girl—Tim McGraw (country)
4. Daddy's Angel—T. Carter (Wedding/Country)
5. I Believe in Happy Endings—Neil Diamond (vocalists)
6. Because You Loved Me—Celine Dion (vocalists)
7. Daddy's Little Girl—Michael Buble (vocalists)
8. Butterfly Kisses—Bob Carlisle (Christian)
9. Daughters—John Mayer (pop)
10. Dad, You're My Hero—Teresa James (wedding)
11. My Little Girl—Steve Kirwan (wedding)
12. Somewhere Over the Rainbow—"Iz" (Acoustic/Hawaiian)
13. Look to the Rainbow—Astrud Gilberto (Brazilian/Int'l)
14. Tu Guardian—Juanes (Latin)
15. You Raise Me Up—Josh Groban (classical)
16. Unforgettable—Natalie Cole/Nat King Cole (wedding classic)
17. Daddy—Beyonce (R&B)
18. Ballerina Girl—Lionel Ritchie (80s ballad)
19. Isn't She Lovely—Stevie Wonder (soul) (note: I recommend editing out the intro section with crying baby!)
20. My Girl—The Temptations (Motown/Soul)

V. Mother-Son Dance

1. Stand By Me—Ben E. King (soul)
2. I'll Always Love My Mama—The Intruders (R&B/Soul)
3. Singing a Song for My Mother—Bohannon (R&B/Soul)
4. A Song for Mama—Boyz II Men (R&B/Soul)
5. You Raise Me Up—Josh Groban (classical)
6. Close to You—The Carpenters (soft rock)
7. Child of Mine—Carole King (folk)
8. Song for My Son—Mikki Viereck (wedding)
9. It Happens in a Heartbeat—Teresa James (wedding)
10. The Man You've Become—Molly Pasutti (wedding)
11. You've Got a Friend in Me—Randy Newman with Lyle Lovett (Disney)
12. The Wind Beneath My Wings—Bette Midler (vocalist)
13. All to You—DJ Keo (country)
14. My Wish—Rascal Flatts (country)
15. I Hope You Dance—LeAnn Womack (country)
16. Through the Years—Kenny Rogers (country)
17. Forever Young—Alphaville (80s)
18. Can't Smile Without You—Barry Manilow (vocalist)
19. Simple Man—Lynrd Skynrd (southern rock)
20. What a Wonderful World—Louis Armstrong (classic)
21. A Mother's Song—T. Carter (Wedding/Country)

VI. Cakecutting Songs

1. Sugar, Sugar—The Archies (oldies)
2. Chapel of Love—The Dixie Cups (oldies)
3. Theme from The Good, the Bad and the Ugly—Ennio Morricone (soundtracks)
4. Hit Me With Your Best Shot—Pat Benatar (80s)
5. I Want Candy—The Bow Wow Wow (80s)

The BRIDE'S GUIDE to Selecting the Perfect Wedding DJ

6. Pour Some Sugar on Me—Def Leppard (80s rock)
7. Lips Like Sugar—Echo & the Bunnymen (80s/New Wave)
8. Silly Love Songs—Paul McCartney (pop)
9. How Sweet It Is (To Be Loved by You)—Marvin Gaye or James Taylor (R&B/soft rock)
10. For Once in My Life—Stevie Wonder (R&B)
11. I Can't Help Myself (Sugar Pie, Honey Bunch)—The Four Tops (Motown)
12. When I'm 64—The Beatles (pop)
13. Cut the Cake—Average White Band (disco)
14. Wanna Grow Old with You—Adam Sandler (soundtrack)
15. Super Mario Brothers Theme Song (soundtrack)
16. Eat It—'Weird Al' Yankovic (song parody)
17. Candy Man—Christina Aguilera (pop)
18. Marry You—Bruno Mars (pop)
19. I Do—Colbie Caillat (pop)
20. Truly, Madly, Deeply—Savage Garden (pop ballad)
21. Sugar—Flo Rida (dance)
22. Firecracker—Josh Turner (country)
23. Say Hey, I Love You—Michael Franti (dance)
24. My Favourite Book—Stars (alternative)
25. No One's Gonna Love You—Band of Horses (alternative)
26. Rain or Shine—Matthew Perryman Jones (rock)
27. Love and Marriage—Frank Sinatra (vocalist)
28. It Had to Be You—Harry Connick, Jr. (big band/vocalist)
29. Ice Cream—Sara McLachlan (vocalist)
30. L-O-V-E—Nat King Cole (vocalist)
31. Gymnopedies No. 1— Erik Satie (classical/soundtrack)
32. The Sweetest Love—Robin Thicke (R&B)
33. P.D.A. (We Just Don't Care)—John Legend (R&B)
34. By Your Side—Sade (R&B)
35. Spin Spin Sugar (Armand Van Helden Remix)—Sneaker Pimps (electronic)

VII. 50 Songs for a Wedding (2013 Edition)

The following selections may change from year to year. Here in the Northeast, these selections generally "get the people going." I've included a variety of cocktail hour, dinner music, ballads, oldies and modern dance music. A broad mix is desirable at most weddings, as it unites guests of all ages.

1. Quando, Quando, Quando—Michael Buble with Nelly Furtado (cocktail hour/dinner)
2. Our Day Will Come—Amy Winehouse (cocktail/dinner)
3. Beyond the Sea—Bobby Darin (oldies)
4. Runaround Sue—Dion (oldies)
5. Twist & Shout—The Beatles (oldies/rock)
6. Shout (Parts 1 and 2)—The Isley Brothers (oldies)
7. Chapel of Love—The Dixie Cups (oldies)
8. Marry You—Bruno Mars (pop)
9. In the Mood—Glen Miller Band (big band)
10. That's Amore—Dean Martin (oldies)
11. My Girl—The Temptations (Motown)
12. Sign, Sealed, Delivered, I'm Yours—Stevie Wonder (Motown)
13. Baby I Need Your Loving—The Four Tops (Motown)
14. Ain't No Mountain High Enough—Marvin Gaye (Motown)
15. What You Won't Do for Love—Bobby Caldwell (R&B)
16. Blurred Lines—Robin Thicke w/ Pharell and T.I. (R&B)
17. Yeah!—Usher with Lil' Jon (party starter)
18. Single Ladies—Beyonce (R&B)
19. Empire State of Mind—Jay-Z with Alicia Keys (hip hop)
20. Got To Be Real—Cheryl Lynn (disco)
21. That's the Way I Like It—K.C. & the Sunshine Band (disco)
22. Play That Funky Music—Wild Cherry (disco)
23. Get Lucky—Daft Punk (electronic/party starter)

24. Push It—Salt n' Pepa (80s)
25. Could You Be Loved—Bob Marley (reggae)
26. I Can't Wait—Nu-Shooz (freestyle/party starter)
27. Rock Your Body—Justin Timberlake (pop/party starter)
28. It Takes Two—DJ Rob Base and EZ Rock (90s)
29. Jump Around—House of Pain (90s)
30. Asi Es La Mujer—Victor Manuelle (salsa)
31. Addicted to You—Shakira (merengue)
32. The Harlem Shake—Baauer (trap/novelty)
33. Gangnam Style—Psy (international/open dancing)
34. One More Time—Daft Punk (open dancing)
35. Party Rock Anthem—LMFAO (open dancing)
36. Wanna Be Startin' Somethin'—Michael Jackson (dance)
37. Danza Kuduro—Don Omar (open dancing/Latin)
38. Calle Ocho (I Know You Want Me)—Pitbull (open dance/Latin)
39. Red Solo Cup—Toby Keith (country)
40. Rattle—Bingo Players (house/electro)
41. Cupid Shuffle—Cupid (line dance)
42. Cha-Cha Slide—DJ Casper (line dance)
43. The Wobble—V.I.C. (line dance)
44. Unforgettable—Natalie Cole (ballad)
45. Unchained Melody—The Righteous Brothers (ballad)
46. The Way You Look Tonight—Frank Sinatra (ballad)
47. You are the Best Thing—Ray LaMontagne (ballad)
48. Let's Stay Together—Al Green (ballad)
49. You Shook Me All Night Long—AC/DC (rock)
50. In Da Club (clean version)—50 Cent (hip hop)

Website Links

The websites compiled below, some of which were referenced in the text, may be of further assistance in your quest to find the perfect wedding DJ and select songs for your special day!

Review Sites

www.WeddingWire.com

www.WeddingChannel.com

www.Yelp.com

Sites to Research Wedding DJs (and other Vendors)

www.google.com

www.bing.com

www.yahoo.com

www.YouTube.com

www.WeDJ.com

www.ADJA.org

www.NJDJN.org

www.njwedding.com

www.wedalert.com

www.livemusicconsulting.com

www.gigmasters.com

www.partyblast.com

Sites with Song Ideas and Playlists

www.weddingmusiccentral.com

www.myweddingmusic.com

www.wedding-music-help.com

www.vitaminstringquartet.com

www.mobilebeat.com/top-200/

www.digitaldreamdoor.com/

http://www.elegantmoods.net/

www.hudsonvalleyharpist.com/ceremonysuggestions.htm

General Wedding Planning Websites

www.theknot.com

www.Pinterest.com

www.weddingbee.com

www.topweddingsites.com

Connect with DJ Gregg Ambient

www.ambientdj.com (website)

www.Facebook.com/AmbientDJ (Facebook)

www.Twitter.com/AmbientDJs (Twitter)

www.instagram.com./AmbientDJs

http://pinterest.com/greggambient/ (Pinterest)

http://ambientdj.com/ambience-a-nj-dj-blog/ (Blog)

www.WeDJ.com

www.ADJA.org

www.NJDJN.org

www.njwedding.com

www.wedalert.com

www.livemusicconsulting.com

www.gigmasters.com

www.partyblast.com

Sites with Song Ideas and Playlists

www.weddingmusiccentral.com

www.myweddingmusic.com

www.wedding-music-help.com

www.vitaminstringquartet.com

www.mobilebeat.com/top-200/

www.digitaldreamdoor.com/

http://www.elegantmoods.net/

www.hudsonvalleyharpist.com/ceremonysuggestions.htm

General Wedding Planning Websites

www.theknot.com

www.Pinterest.com

www.weddingbee.com

www.topweddingsites.com

Connect with DJ Gregg Ambient

www.ambientdj.com (website)

www.Facebook.com/AmbientDJ (Facebook)

www.Twitter.com/AmbientDJs (Twitter)

www.instagram.com./AmbientDJs

http://pinterest.com/greggambient/ (Pinterest)

http://ambientdj.com/ambience-a-nj-dj-blog/ (Blog)

Closing

Thank you for purchasing my book, "The BRIDE's GUIDE to Selecting the Perfect Wedding DJ." I hope you found the tips useful and are now well on your way to finding your wedding DJ!

If you found this book useful, please review it on Amazon.com. Reviews are hard for authors to earn, and I would sincerely appreciate your help!

Please don't hesitate to email me at: gregg@ambientdj.com with any additional questions about the process of researching and interviewing wedding DJs. If you are planning a wedding in New Jersey, New York or Eastern Pennsylvania, I would be delighted to speak with you about performing at your wedding.

Musically yours,

DJ Gregg Ambient

About the Author

Gregg Hollmann, better known as **"DJ Gregg Ambient"** is a lifelong music lover who parlayed a passion for music and parties into a career. As a high school student, he played piano, tuba and alto saxophone and feverishly collected records—particularly jazz LPs. Attending The College of New Jersey (TCNJ), including a year spent abroad in Japan at Kansai Gaidai University, he graduated Magna Cum Laude with a degree in Finance. Gregg then worked for Merrill Lynch covering the Asia-Pacific markets, and later for Caspian Securities in Manila, Philippines as a food & beverage analyst.

Returning to the U.S. in the late '90s, he reconnected with his passion for music and began experimenting as a DJ, initially playing house parties for friends. Inspired by attending his sister's wedding, he invested in his first professional DJ sound system in 2003 and began booking parties under his new company "Ambient DJ Service."

Since then, Ambient DJ Service has quickly grown to become one of the top providers of wedding DJ entertainment in Central New Jersey. Ambient DJ Service is a four- year consecutive winner of the WeddingWire "Bride's Choice Award" and a 2013 winner of The Knot's prestigious "Best of Weddings" award in the category of Disc Jockeys. Ambient DJ Service was also voted "Best Disc Jockey Service in New Jersey" in the 2013 Wedding Industry Expert Awards. Gregg performs at over 200 events a year.

Gregg currently serves as the President of New Jersey's largest and premier association of professional mobile disc jockeys, the New Jersey Disc Jockey Network (NJDJN).

To learn more about Gregg and Ambient DJ Service, you can connect with him at:

www.ambientdj.com (Website)

www.facebook.com/AmbientDJ (Facebook)

www.twitter.com/AmbientDJs (Twitter)

www.instagram.com/AmbientDJs

Made in the USA
Middletown, DE
02 February 2016